America's favorite comfort food

Glorious grits

by Susan McEwen McIntosh

Oxmoor House®

America's favorite comfort food

Glorious grits

by Susan McEwen McIntosh

To my parents,

Peggy and Ralph McEwen

Oxmoor
House.

ISBN-13: 978-0-8487-3291-2
ISBN-10: 0-8487-3291-X
Library of Congress Control Number: 2009925689

Printed in the United States of America
First Printing 2009

To order additional publications, call 1-800-765-6400.

For more books to enrich your life, visit **oxmoorhouse.com**

To search, savor, and share thousands of recipes, visit **myrecipes.com**

Cover: Old-Fashioned Grits (page 18)
Page 2: Pecan-Grits Pie (page 157)

Oxmoor House, Inc.
VP, Publishing Director: Jim Childs
Executive Editor: Susan Payne Dobbs
Brand Manager: Daniel Fagan
Managing Editor: L. Amanda Owens

Glorious Grits—America's Favorite Comfort Food
Author: Susan McEwen McIntosh
Editor: Kelly Hooper Troiano
Project Editor: Vanessa Lynn Rusch
Senior Designer: Melissa Jones Clark
Director, Test Kitchens: Elizabeth Tyler Austin
Assistant Director, Test Kitchens: Julie Christopher
Test Kitchens Professionals: Jane Chambliss,
  Kathleen Royal Phillips, Catherine Crowell Steele,
  Ashley T. Strickland, Deborah Wise
Photography Director: Jim Bathie
Senior Photo Stylist: Kay E. Clarke
Associate Photo Stylist: Katherine Eckert Coyne
Production Manager: Tamara Nall

Contributors
Copy Editor: Dolores Hydock
Project Editor: Emily Chappell
Indexer: Mary Ann Laurens
Interns: Georgia Dodge, Christine Taylor,
  Angela Valente
Food Stylists: Ana Price Kelly, Debby Maugans
Photographers: Beau Gustafson, Lee Harrelson,
  John T. McIntosh
Editorial Contributor: Leigh McIntosh

contents

foreword

Finally we have a book that celebrates the milled grain that my four boys crave every morning. The popularity of grits in the Besh House is not limited to Brendan, Jack, Luke, and Andrew, though, because for generations, members of our family have sustained themselves on the glorious grit. Through the Civil War, the Great Depression, the Second World War, and devastating natural disasters, the glorious grit gave sustenance to both body and soul through dishes as varied as shrimp and grits, busters and grits, grits and gravy, grillades and grits, baked grits, fried grits, cheese grits, and just plain old-fashioned grits.

Over the years, grits didn't just fill our plates—it filled our conversation, too, with stories about our grandmothers, wives, mimies, grannies, and grand mèrers, and how those resourceful women used the glorious grit to tie together the flavors of thick and salty bacon, smoked sausages, rich gravies, and sweet backstrap molasses.

The glory days of grits, though, are hardly in the past. Today's grits are better then ever, thanks to our friends at the McEwen & Sons gristmill and other millers who make it possible to find high-quality, whole-grain, stone-ground grits. In a fast-paced world where everything changes, it's comforting to know that this simple, nutritious, and delicious food continues to sustain and delight new generations of people who love grits—in all their glory.

It's comforting to know that this simple, nutritious, and delicious food continues to sustain and delight new generations of people who love grits.

–John Besh, Chef and Owner
Restaurant August, Lüke, Besh
Steak, and La Provençe

introduction

Most Southerners consider grits the ultimate comfort food—simple, hearty, and satisfying. So I love hearing that enlightened chefs in the South and across the country are creating grits dishes that are innovative, incredibly delicious, and on-the-plate gorgeous—in fact, grits today are glorious!

My Southern affection for grits was heightened by a career focused on food. I've consumed many spoonfuls of grits, especially while sampling and writing about Southern food for *Southern Living* magazine. And as a registered dietitian and author of the first *Cooking Light Cookbook*, I understand and appreciate the nutritional value of grits and other whole grains in our diets.

But my personal passion for grits was inspired by my brother, Frank McEwen, whose gristmill grinds organic corn into stone-ground grits, cornmeal, and polenta for discriminating chefs and home cooks nationwide. When he started his corn-grinding business, Frank asked me to develop some basic recipes for his customers—that request became the seed for *Glorious Grits*. Since then, I've interviewed many progressive chefs and have experimented with their secrets for transforming grits, cornmeal, and polenta from simple comfort foods into glorious components of fine dining. What you have in your hands is a bit of history, a brief human interest story, a guide to finding really good grits, and a collection of delicious recipes from my own kitchen and from the kitchens of some of the best chefs in the country. Now you can discover *Glorious Grits* for yourself!

Susan McEwen McIntosh

I've interviewed many progressive chefs and have experimented with their secrets for transforming grits, cornmeal, and polenta from simple comfort foods into glorious components of fine dining.

—Susan McEwen McIntosh

We Southerners love our grits, and have for centuries. When European explorers landed on our continent, Native Americans were already grinding their plentiful harvest of corn into a coarse meal that they boiled and ate year-round. The new settlers quickly learned to depend on ground corn, in the form of cornmeal and

grits in the new south

grits, for survival during those early days. Grits have come a long way since then, and the South's favorite grain is rapidly gaining popularity throughout the country as many of today's top chefs and home cooks reinvent this simple, soothing grain into glorious, sophisticated dishes.

The South Gets a New Gristmill

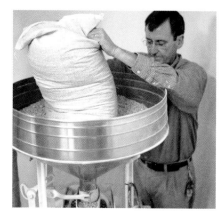

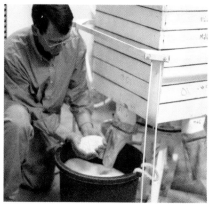

Although today's electricity-powered gristmills are not as picturesque as the older water-turned mills, they more efficiently turn out old-fashioned meal and grits. Here, Frank McEwen pours dried organic corn into his stone burr gristmill in Wilsonville, Alabama. The corn is crushed as it passes through large rotating stones, and then the ground corn is sifted through a wire screen to produce grits, polenta, and cornmeal.

It may be surprising that in today's world of mass food production the owners of a modern hardware and farm-supply store would start grinding grits the old-fashioned stone-ground way. The family business was already bustling in the late 90s as my brother and father catered to farmers as well as visitors from nearby Birmingham at Coosa Valley Milling Company's hardware store and feed mill in Wilsonville, Alabama. Two seemingly unrelated events converged to get the grinding started for the birth of McEwen & Sons grits.

First, my parents traveled to Smoky Mountain National Park and visited an old-fashioned water-turned gristmill at picturesque Cades Cove. While there, they learned that the gift shop's inventory of stone-ground products was supplemented by a hardware store in nearby Sevierville, Tennessee. They were impressed enough to bring each of us children souvenir bags of stone-ground grits and cornmeal. Daddy's special gift to Frank was an idea: "Why don't you buy a gristmill to grind and sell grits at the store?" Frank replied, "We'll see."

A bit later, a health scare put Frank in the hospital for several days and transformed him into what my sister, Ann, and I lovingly called "a health food snob." Frank's health problem was resolved, and in an effort to proactively improve their health, Frank and his wife, Helen, along with their two young sons, embraced an organic, high-fiber diet. But they had trouble finding organic grits and cornmeal at the local grocery. "I guess I'll just have to grind my own," Frank declared.

The grinding begins

Frank remembered Daddy's gristmill idea and started searching for sources of organic corn. But how could he justify the purchase of an expensive gristmill to grind corn just for his family of four? Ever the entrepreneurs, Frank and Helen decided that if they were interested in organic grits and cornmeal, others would be, too. The gristmill was purchased and the grinding began.

To kick-start the new business, Frank boldly delivered sample bags of grits to some of the most notable names in the Birmingham, Alabama, restaurant business. Several days later, he got a phone call from Frank Stitt, Owner and Chef of three award-winning Birmingham restaurants. Chef Stitt had tried the grits in his signature grits appetizer at Highlands Bar and Grill, loved that the grits were organic, and wanted more. Chefs talk, and word spread—soon other restaurants in Birmingham and across the Southeast added McEwen & Sons grits to their menus.

With the gristmill in full swing, Frank was soon delivering dozens of family-size 2-pound bags to local groceries, and much larger 10-pound bags to popular Birmingham restaurants like Highlands Bar and Grill, Hot and Hot Fish Club, Little Savannah, and Standard Bistro. He even started grinding polenta at the request of a couple of chefs at Italian restaurants in town. Many of Frank's customers in Wilsonville had never heard of polenta, but once they realized that polenta was a close cousin to grits and cornmeal, they gave it a try.

Southern grits go national

Today Frank ships grits, polenta, and cornmeal to fine restaurants across the country. He sells products over the internet and by mail-order, but he prefers the one-on-one approach so that he can talk with customers over the phone and ask where they heard about his grits. One caller declared, "Send me some grits—we're gritless in Arkansas!" And a notable Italian chef in Atlanta told Frank, "This is the best polenta I've eaten since I left Italy."

While I'm certainly most fond of the grits, polenta, and cornmeal that feature the McEwen & Sons label on the package, I'm acquainted with other gristmills that grind corn the old-fashioned stone-ground way, as well. I've listed those in the index along with their contact information (see page 172 for a "Grits Trail Map"). If you want the freshest grits available, give one of those businesses a call or a visit while traveling.

a three-generation business

The name "McEwen & Sons" includes three generations involved in producing and selling organic products. While my brother, Frank, handles the grain-grinding responsibilities, my father works with grandsons Frank, Jr. and Luke to provide the ideal accompaniment to cooked grits: big, fresh, organic brown and blue eggs. The boys raise hundreds of hens in a free-range environment and feed the chickens only all-natural feed containing no antibiotics, hormones, or animal protein. With the dedicated help of grandfather "Papa Ralph," Frank, Jr. and Luke gather and crate the eggs to sell to many of the same restaurants that serve McEwen & Sons grits and polenta.

Grits "Reinvented"

Breakfast in some parts of the country might include hot oatmeal or Cream of Wheat, but we Southerners grew up with simple, soothing grits—comfort food at its best. In fact, grits have nourished and comforted our ancestors for centuries. In summers past, industrious farmers picked corn to eat fresh during the summer and to dry and grind into grits and cornmeal for nourishment year-round. Back then, a bowl of grits was not sophisticated—it was common, and it was sustenance.

In recent years, Southern foods in general—and grits in particular—have been incredibly transformed. Notable chefs, such as Alabama-born Frank Stitt, use grits as an artist uses a blank canvas to create culinary masterpieces, stunning both in appearance and flavor (see page 40). Frank Stitt is an example of a Southern chef who has embraced humble, tradi-tional Southern food, caressed it with sophisticated culinary techniques, and won national acclaim in the process. In the creative hands of Frank and other progressive chefs, grits now play a major role in every part of the menu at restaurants from coast to coast.

Welcome to the South!

Gary Donlick, who served as Executive Chef at Pano's and Paul's, claims he never ate grits until he married a Southern girl and moved to Atlanta. He says that he especially never understood grits for breakfast, but after enjoy-ing grits with his wife's family over holidays and experimenting with his own flavorings and pairings of grits with signature entrées, he's become a convert. "When a grits dish is done right, it's really delicious," Gary says. In fact, one of his favorite recipes combines Berkshire pork, caramelized onions, baby carrots, and Parmesan grits.

At Sambuca in Houston, Chef Steve Wasserman adds Cajun flavor to grits, agreeing with Gary that the seasoning matters most in great grits recipes. Steve's signature is adding sautéed andouille sausage, green onions, and smoked Gouda to grits, and then smothering the grits in crawfish sauce.

Grits from coast to coast

Talented "reinventers" cook up grits in surprising new ways at restaurants from coast to coast. Napa Valley Chef Nick Heinrich spoons up cream-laden grits as a base for grilled portobello mushrooms and rich Bordelaise sauce (see page 56). And when Chef Brian Williams lived in Philmont, New York, he created a mouthwatering main dish of bay scallops with oyster mushrooms in a savory shallot- and thyme-scented wine sauce spooned atop a foundation of simple grits (see page 107). Fellow Chef David Wurth explained the popularity of the entrée among Local 111 restaurant guests in Philmont: "Southern transplants who taste our grits prepared with various accompaniments feel reconnected to some glorious lost flavors."

When asked what people outside of the South think about grits, Brian explained to me, "Polenta has been a long-time favorite of New Yorkers, and until now grits never became popular. I believe it is because we never before had access to a high-quality product. Thanks to purveyors of stone-ground grits, we now enjoy what Southerners have loved for generations." Like Brian and other innovative chefs, John Norman, of Destin, Florida, insists that stone-ground grits make a real difference in the success of his recipes (see page 113). John says that unlike commercially ground quick grits, stone-ground grits have "the flavor and aroma of fresh corn."

Grits in all their glory

I realized that grits had truly been reinvented when I saw chefs pairing the stone-ground variety of this simple, historically inexpensive grain with the most expensive of ingredients. One delightful example is the marriage of creamy cooked grits with the rare black truffle, a combination created by Chef Mark Hibbs at his award-winning restaurant, Ratcliffe On the Green, in Charlotte, North Carolina (see page 126). Mark starts with organic grits from nearby Anson Mills in Columbia, South Carolina, who, like McEwen & Sons, provide cooks nationwide with the perfect canvas of fresh stone-ground grits for the culinary masterpieces you can create yourself.

"Grits on the Green"

...The real highlight of the meal was, as hoped, the side order of Black Truffle Grits. I'm not the kind of girl who likes things simply because everyone else does, and I was skeptical about how great these grits would really be. But after one small bite, I was stunned. The complex flavor was immediately unforgettable yet not overpowering. Immersed in the rich flavor of this small dish, I felt surprisingly satisfied and full. It was as if these grits had been created with me in mind, as if they had been my favorite food for years. The combination of timeless grits and rare, earthy truffles filled me with warmth and a longing to slow time so that I might savor both the ambiance of the restaurant and the depth of the food. As you can guess, these Black Truffle Grits were unlike anything I have ever tasted....

Leigh M. McIntosh,
Uptown Magazine

It all begins with corn. Cooks in the southern United States pour dried, coarsely ground corn into boiling water to make grits, while in other parts of the country a more finely ground form of corn becomes polenta. When a miller grinds dried corn even more finely

grits, polenta & cornmeal

into a flourlike meal, he creates cornmeal. But all grits, polenta, and cornmeal are not equal, and the following pages explain why. Take a new look at old-fashioned grits, polenta, and cornmeal. They're whole grain, stone ground, and sometimes even organic—comfort food at its best!

Whole Grain Goodness

Whole grains are getting a lot of attention these days. Studies show that eating whole grains lowers the risk of stroke, Type 2 diabetes, and heart disease, and may help with weight maintenance. Eating three or more servings daily gives the greatest health benefit, but some studies show that any amount helps in disease prevention.

Grains are considered "whole" when all three parts of the original seed (also called kernel) are present. The **bran** (hull) is the high-fiber outer layer, which is rich in antioxidants and B vitamins. The **germ,** just under the outer skin, contains B vitamins, some protein, and healthy fats, and delivers a hearty, rich flavor when cooked. The **endosperm** contains carbohydrates and some protein but little fiber and only small amounts of other nutrients.

When corn and other grains are milled conventionally at large processing plants, the bran and germ of the grain are usually removed, leaving only the carbohydrate-rich endosperm. The bran and germ are used in the production of various products such as cereal, corn oil, and animal feed. Since the germ contains fat, removing it allows the degerminated grain product to last longer on the shelf without refrigeration. This boosts profitability for the food manufacturers, but sacrifices flavor and nutrients for the consumer.

Why stone ground?

Many culinary and nutrition experts believe that the grits, polenta, and cornmeal ground in stone burr gristmills provide more flavor and nutritional value than those produced in modern mills. In this old-fashioned method of grinding, the corn passes between two granite stones that crush and grind the grain slowly, generating a lower temperature than occurs in modern milling. Modern roller milling results in a longer shelf life when the product sits at room temperature, but there is a cost: Important vitamins and other nutrients are lost in the process.

Corn and other whole grains are rich in vitamins, minerals, antioxidants, and fiber. Health experts recommend that we eat three or more servings of whole grains daily.

Why organic?

When a food is labeled "100% Organic" you can be sure that no toxic chemicals were used in its growing and processing. Only a few gristmills nationwide produce stone-ground grits, polenta, and cornmeal—even fewer follow the strict U.S. Department of Agriculture standards required to label their products as 100% organic. While many culinary experts claim that organic products taste better, the most convincing argument for many families may be their desire to avoid unnecessary pesticides and other chemicals in their quest for healthful living and eating.

Cooking tips

Keep in mind the following tips when using stone-ground grits, polenta, and cornmeal in your own favorite recipes:

1. Stone-ground grits take longer to cook than the quick-cooking variety—just how long depends on how coarse or fine the grain. Refer to the cooking instructions on the package label, and adjust your recipe accordingly. You can cut the cooking time for coursely ground grits by soaking the dry grits in water overnight before cooking.

2. Stone-ground grits require frequent stirring to release the starch and keep the grits from clumping and sticking to the bottom of the pan.

3. Blue, white, and yellow stone-ground grits, polenta, and cornmeal can be used interchangeably in most recipes. Yellow and blue corn products are thought to be a little sweeter and more flavorful than white.

4. Whole-grain products still contain the nutrient-rich germ, which is perishable at room temperature. Be sure to refrigerate or freeze stone-ground, whole-grain grits, polenta, and cornmeal soon after purchase.

5. You can easily remove the dry husks found in stone-ground grits if the husks are too "gritty" for your taste. Just pour water over the dry grits in a pan. Let the grits stand in the water for a few minutes, allowing the husks to float to the top. Using a small wire strainer, skim off and discard the husks.

McEwen & Sons Gristmill in Wilsonville, Alabama, and Anson Mills in Columbia, South Carolina, produce exclusively organic grains. For a complete list of gristmills that feature stone-ground products, turn to page 173.

Old-Fashioned Grits

Here's a basic recipe for stone-ground grits. As with all the recipes in this cookbook, the grits we used were done after 20 to 25 minutes. However, the cooking time will vary depending on how coarsely or finely ground the grain.

Many of the chefs I interviewed said that they prefer to cook their grits early in the day, then leave the pot over very low heat for at least an hour—even all afternoon—stirring occasionally and adding more liquid along the way to keep the grits at the desired consistency.

garlic tip
For an easy dose of flavor, drop 1 or 2 peeled garlic cloves into the pan with the uncooked grits. After cooking the grits, you can remove and discard the garlic.

4	cups water
1	teaspoon salt
1	cup uncooked stone-ground grits

2	tablespoons butter
¼	teaspoon freshly ground black pepper

Bring water and salt to a boil in a medium, heavy saucepan; gradually whisk in grits. Reduce heat; simmer, uncovered, 20 to 25 minutes or until thick, stirring often. Remove from heat; stir in butter and pepper. Garnish with thyme, if desired. **Yield:** 4 to 6 servings.

For 2 to 3 servings: Follow above directions, using 2 cups water, ½ teaspoon salt, ½ cup uncooked stone-ground grits, 1 tablespoon butter, and ⅛ teaspoon black pepper. The cook time remains the same.

Slow-Cooker Grits

I've prepared a lot of grits, and some of my kitchen's creamiest grits came from a slow cooker. It's not often that a slow cooker is the best choice for cooking grits— my slow cooker is a 4-quart version, and I rarely need that large a quantity of grits. However, if I'm preparing grits for a dinner party and need a hefty supply, this slow-cooker version can be the perfect way to go. It uses a lower percentage of water since there's less evaporation.

3	cups uncooked stone-ground grits	1	tablespoon salt
6	tablespoons butter, melted	9	cups hot water

Place grits in a 4-quart slow cooker, and stir in butter and salt; whisk in water. Cover and cook on HIGH for 3 hours, stirring after 2 hours. **Yield:** 12 to 14 servings.

Overnight Grits

Soaking grits overnight softens them and reduces their cook time almost by half.

3	cups water	1	teaspoon salt
1	cup uncooked stone-ground grits	2	tablespoons butter

Combine water and grits in a medium, heavy saucepan; cover and let stand overnight. Add salt to grits, and bring to a boil, stirring constantly. Reduce heat; simmer, uncovered, 12 to 15 minutes or until thick, stirring often. **Yield:** 4 to 6 servings.

colorful grits

Many long-time grits-loving Southerners would be surprised to learn that grits come in colors other than white. Yellow grits have a stronger corn flavor than traditional white grits and also provide more vitamin A than the white. But the milder taste of white grits may some-times be preferred, depending on the seasoning or sauce.

Some gristmills sell a yellow-and-white combination called speckled grits (pictured on opposite page) for those who have a difficult time deciding on a color of choice (see page 102).

For an unexpected splash of color on your plate, follow Chef Clif Holt's lead and cook up some blue grits (see pages 120 and 137). You'll get an extra dose of nutrition since blue corn contains lysine and is higher in protein than yellow or white corn.

Grits cakes

If you're looking for a unique way to present grits, plan ahead and make grits cakes. Several of the recipes in this book feature a version of grits or polenta cakes. After lots of testing, I came up with some helpful tips for making the cakes successfully.

In order for stone-ground grits cakes to firm up sufficiently, coarsely ground grits need to be cooked completely to a very tender stage. In fact, it's best to combine the uncooked grits with cold water in the pan, and then bring the water to a boil (stirring constantly). This procedure brings out the starchiness of the grain, making it somewhat stickier, and is especially important when moist ingredients such as corn or onions are stirred into the grits mixture.

Before chilling the cooked grits mixture, it sometimes helps to place a dry paper towel over the cooked grits. The towel absorbs condensation that forms on the grits as they chill and helps ensure that the patties hold together while they are cooked, broiled, or grilled.

to make grits cakes:

1. Chill grits thoroughly until firm before removing from the pan. Cut chilled grits into desired shapes.

2. Cook grits cakes on the grill, in a skillet, or in the oven.

Quick-and-Easy Polenta

The cooking methods for polenta and grits are similar. Because of its finer grain, polenta cooks to the tender, done stage more quickly. You can serve polenta plain as in Quick-and-Easy Polenta, add sautéed vegetables as in Colorful Polenta (pictured below; recipe on page 140), or chill it for cutting into shapes as described on the following page.

4	cups water	1	cup uncooked stone-ground polenta
1	teaspoon salt	1	tablespoon butter

Bring water and salt to a boil in a medium, heavy saucepan; gradually whisk in polenta. Reduce heat; simmer, uncovered, 12 to 14 minutes or until thick, stirring often. Remove from heat; add butter, and stir until butter melts. **Yield:** 4 to 6 servings.

grits vs polenta

Even we Southerners recognize that polenta has a much more pleasant-sounding name than grits. Still, our ancestors would never have asked for a bowl of polenta for breakfast, and I'm sure that children in Italy never asked for grits. So is the difference merely language and latitude? The difference between grits and polenta is the size of the ground kernels, which results in a difference in the cooked texture. The ground corn that becomes polenta passes through a smaller-holed screen than the corn that becomes grits. As a result, the polenta cooks more quickly and into a smoother texture than you'll get with stone-ground grits.

Sliced Polenta

For a shapely presentation, prepare sliced polenta or polenta cakes. The fine texture of polenta firms up nicely, making it especially easy to slice and cook on the stovetop, in the oven, or on the grill.

Spoon about 3 cups cooked seasoned polenta (made from 1 cup uncooked polenta) into an 8- x 4-inch loaf pan lined with heavy-duty plastic wrap, spreading evenly; let cool 15 minutes. (If polenta is still warm, cover with a dry paper towel.) Cover pan, and chill polenta 2 hours or until very firm. Turn chilled polenta out onto a cutting board (photo 1). Remove plastic wrap from polenta, and cut polenta into ½-inch slices (photo 2).

To make other shapes, spoon polenta into an 11- x 7-inch dish lined with heavy-duty plastic wrap. Proceed as directed above. Remove polenta from dish; cut into shapes with a knife or cookie cutter.

To panfry slices, melt butter in a large skillet; add polenta slices, and cook 5 minutes on each side or until lightly browned.

To bake, place polenta slices on a baking sheet coated with cooking spray. Bake at 425° for 20 minutes; flip slices, and bake 15 more minutes or until lightly browned.

To grill, place polenta slices on a grill rack coated with cooking spray; grill, covered with grill lid, over medium-high heat (350° to 400°) until lightly browned on both sides.

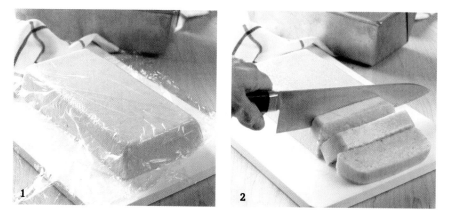

1   2

Self-Rising Cornmeal

Many favorite Southern recipes, especially those for cornbread, call for self-rising cornmeal. As with self-rising flour, the leavening and salt are already mixed with the meal. Use these proportions when your recipe calls for self-rising cornmeal.

1   cup stone-ground cornmeal   ½   teaspoon salt
1½ teaspoons baking powder

Combine all ingredients in a bowl until well blended. Cover tightly, and store in refrigerator. Use in recipes calling for self-rising cornmeal. **Yield:** 1 cup.

Variation for about 6 cups self-rising cornmeal: Combine 6 cups plain cornmeal, 3 tablespoons baking powder, and 1 tablespoon salt in a bowl until well blended. Cover tightly, and store in refrigerator.

sifting stone-ground cornmeal

Stone-ground cornmeal from some gristmills may contain more large grains and flecks of husks than you'd like for some recipes, especially desserts. Buying finely ground cornmeal (sometimes called "bolted cornmeal") may solve this dilemma, or you can gently sift the cornmeal through a wire strainer to remove some of those large pieces before measuring the meal.

Whether drizzled with red-eye gravy or married with cheese in a creamy casserole, grits are synonymous with breakfast in the Deep South. And lest you think grits should only be savory,

breakfast & brunch

here's a new idea: Enjoy grits as a nutritious hot cereal, swirled with peanut butter and honey. From the simplest, steaming bowl to the sophisticated, brunch-style soufflé roll, versatile grits get any day started just right.

Creamy Grits with Ham and Red-Eye Gravy

pictured on page 24

Not all Southerners are born order-ing grits with their morning eggs. In fact, my first taste came in the fifth grade when I stayed overnight with a best friend from school. Her mother served us grits with eggs and biscuits for breakfast, and I thought they were awful. They were bland and mushy, and didn't have much flavor. (It's likely that they were the quick grits version from a box.) In later years, I was introduced to coarsely ground grits, full of texture and real corn flavor, and realized why Southern families have for generations included grits with their morning meals of eggs, country ham, red-eye gravy, and biscuits.

2   cups water
2   cups milk
1   teaspoon salt
1   cup uncooked stone-ground white or yellow grits
1   tablespoon butter
¼   cup half-and-half
½   teaspoon freshly ground black pepper
2   tablespoons butter
1   pound center-cut country ham slices
1½ cups strongly brewed black coffee
1   tablespoon brown sugar

Combine water, milk, and salt in a large, heavy saucepan; cook over medium-high heat just until mixture starts to boil. Gradually whisk in grits. Reduce heat; simmer, uncovered, 20 to 25 minutes or until thick, stirring often. Remove from heat, and stir in 1 tablespoon butter, half-and-half, and pepper; cover and keep warm.

While grits are cooking, melt 2 tablespoons butter in a large cast-iron skillet; add ham. Cook over medium heat 5 to 7 minutes on each side or until browned. Remove ham, reserving drippings in skillet; keep ham warm.

Combine coffee and brown sugar; slowly add to drippings in skillet, stirring to loosen browned particles from bottom of skillet. Bring mixture to a boil; cook, stirring occasionally, until mixture is reduced by half (about 7 minutes).

Serve hot grits with ham and gravy. **Yield:** 4 servings.

Old-Fashioned Grits with Monterey Jack Cheese

4   cups water

1   teaspoon salt

1   cup uncooked stone-ground grits

2   tablespoons butter

1   cup (4 ounces) shredded Monterey Jack cheese

¼   to ½ teaspoon freshly ground black pepper

Bring water and salt to a boil in a medium, heavy saucepan. Gradually whisk in grits. Reduce heat; simmer, uncovered, 20 to 25 minutes or until thick, stirring often. Remove from heat; stir in butter, cheese, and pepper, stirring until cheese melts. **Yield:** 4 servings.

My son, John, loves Cheddar cheese atop his scrambled eggs, but he also loves cheese in his breakfast grits. So instead of doubling up on Cheddar, we often add Monterey Jack cheese to the grits, which makes them especially smooth and rich-tasting.

Breakfast Cheese Grits Casserole

4   cups water

1   teaspoon salt

1   large garlic clove, minced

1   cup uncooked stone-ground grits

1   cup (4 ounces) shredded extra sharp white Cheddar cheese

2   tablespoons butter

1   teaspoon Worcestershire sauce

¼   teaspoon ground red pepper

2   large eggs, lightly beaten

Cooking spray

Bring first 3 ingredients to a boil in a medium, heavy saucepan. Gradually whisk in grits. Reduce heat; simmer, uncovered, 20 to 25 minutes or until thick, stirring often. Remove pan from heat, and stir in cheese and next 3 ingredients.

Preheat oven to 350°. Gradually add beaten eggs to grits mixture; pour into an 11- x 7-inch baking dish coated with cooking spray. Bake, uncovered, at 350° for 45 minutes or until set. **Yield:** 4 to 6 servings.

Every Southern cook has a favorite breakfast grits casserole—here's one that's simple and delicious. Like many grits casseroles, you can cook the grits and assemble the casserole the night before. Just cover and chill the dish overnight, and then pop it in the oven while the coffee is brewing the next morning.

Apple-and-Walnut Grits

Cooking grits in apple juice instead of water provides a fruity flavor that will be a hit with kids.

½ tablespoon butter
1 Granny Smith apple, unpeeled and coarsely chopped
2 cups apple juice
⅛ teaspoon salt
½ cup uncooked stone-ground grits

¼ teaspoon ground cinnamon
2 tablespoons half-and-half
⅛ teaspoon freshly grated nutmeg
¼ cup chopped walnuts or pecans, toasted

Melt butter in a medium, heavy saucepan over medium-high heat; add apple, and sauté 2 to 3 minutes or until apple starts to brown. Add apple juice and salt; bring to a boil. Gradually whisk in grits and cinnamon. Reduce heat; simmer, uncovered, 20 to 25 minutes or until thick, stirring often. Remove from heat; stir in half-and-half and nutmeg. Spoon into bowls, and sprinkle with walnuts. **Yield:** 2 to 3 servings.

Peanut Butter-and-Honey Grits Breakfast Bowl

Think you're partial to grits seasoned with just butter or cheese? Try this recipe to inspire unique flavor combinations. For variety, substitute 2 tablespoons apple butter for the peanut butter and honey.

2 cups nonfat milk
¼ teaspoon salt
½ cup uncooked stone-ground grits

¼ cup chopped dates or raisins
1 tablespoon peanut butter
1 tablespoon honey

Combine milk and salt in a medium, heavy saucepan; cook over medium-high heat just until milk starts to boil. (Be careful as you heat the milk because it can boil out of the pan quickly.) Gradually whisk in grits. Reduce heat; simmer, uncovered, 15 minutes, stirring often. Add dates, and simmer 5 to 10 minutes or until thick, stirring often. Remove from heat, and stir in peanut butter and honey. **Yield:** 2 to 3 servings.

Breakfast Grits and Sausage Casserole

This meaty breakfast casserole is a great way to tell overnight guests that you're happy they came to visit. To make breakfast preparation easier, assemble the casserole the night before. If it's the main dish, count on only 4 servings, but if you're serving it alongside eggs, it's enough for 6 servings.

½   pound hot ground pork sausage
1   (8-ounce) package sliced fresh
    mushrooms
3   cups water
1   teaspoon salt
¾   cup uncooked stone-ground grits

¾   cup (3 ounces) shredded extra sharp
    Cheddar cheese, divided
¼   teaspoon dried thyme
2   large eggs, lightly beaten
Cooking spray

Cook sausage in a large skillet over medium-high heat until browned, stirring to crumble; remove sausage from skillet. Add mushrooms to skillet, and cook 4 minutes or until tender; set sausage and mushrooms aside.

Preheat oven to 350°. Bring water and salt to a boil in a heavy saucepan. Gradually whisk in grits. Reduce heat; simmer, uncovered, 20 to 25 minutes or until thick, stirring often. Remove from heat; stir in ½ cup cheese, thyme, sausage, and mushrooms. Gradually stir in eggs.

Spoon mixture into an 8-inch square baking dish coated with cooking spray. Bake, uncovered, at 350° for 35 minutes or until almost set. Sprinkle with additional ¼ cup cheese, and bake 5 more minutes or until mixture is set and cheese melts. **Yield:** 4 to 6 servings.

yankee grits

After Robin Edelman, a registered dietitian who lives in Vermont, received packages of grits, polenta, and cornmeal from a Southern friend (me), Robin responded with this message, "Re: my first crack at grits—I liked them a lot. I followed the standard recipe subbing Smart Balance buttery spread for the butter, and it worked well. But I'm going to cut back on the butter a tad when I try them again. I've become accustomed to a less buttery taste, and I want the corn taste to predominate. I put pepper into some of them, but then I decided to try some without the pepper and with Vermont maple syrup added. Yum!! I loved them this way and ate the leftovers for breakfast the next day. 'Y'all' are probably cringing to read this—maybe not—and maybe you'll try it with the Vermont maple syrup that I'll send in my goodie package." I did—and I admit that breakfast grits are quite tasty "the Yankee way."

Bacon and Cheddar Cheese Grits Casserole

Mrs. Patsy Riley, First Lady of the State of Alabama

Mrs. Riley says that this recipe may be halved and baked in a 13- x 9-inch baking dish at 350° for 40 minutes or until bubbly. She also recommends fresh herbs (when in season) instead of dried. To avoid extra chopping, she sometimes steeps sprigs of fresh herbs in the milk as it comes to a boil (this takes about 10 minutes). She then removes the herbs from the hot milk, adds the grits, butter, and salt, and cooks the grits as directed before assembling the casserole.

8 cups milk, divided

1 tablespoon salt

2 cups uncooked stone-ground white grits

1 cup unsalted butter

4 large eggs, lightly beaten

2 teaspoons dried dill weed, thyme, or sage or a combination of the three (or 2 tablespoons chopped fresh herbs)

2 cups (8 ounces) shredded Cheddar, Gruyère, or Swiss cheese or a combination of the three, divided

6 slices bacon, cooked until crisp and crumbled

Combine 6 cups milk and salt in a large, heavy saucepan; cook over medium-high heat just until milk starts to boil. Gradually whisk in grits and butter. Reduce heat; simmer, uncovered, 20 to 25 minutes or until thick, stirring often.

Preheat oven to 350°. Remove grits from heat; add remaining 2 cups milk, stirring to cool grits mixture. Stir in eggs, herbs, and 1 cup cheese. Pour grits mixture into a lightly greased 15- x 10-inch baking dish; top with remaining 1 cup cheese. Bake, uncovered, at 350° for 45 minutes or until bubbly. Sprinkle crumbled bacon on top of casserole; serve immediately.
Yield: 14 to 18 servings.

"kiss my grits"

"Miss Patsy," the wife of Alabama's Governor Bob Riley, has spearheaded many fundraising activities to preserve the state's century-old governor's mansion as well as the Hill House, another historic home next door to the executive mansion in Montgomery, Alabama. In February 2008, "Miss Patsy" and Governor Riley invited guests to see the results of the fundraising and to encourage continued giving for the noble cause. The popular and very personable governor's wife named the event, "Kiss My Grits!" The menu included a variety of dishes featuring McEwen & Sons grits prepared by notable chefs from across Alabama. Layers of yellow, white, and blue uncooked grits even filled crystal vases that lined the fireplace mantel and held flowers and candles in place for table centerpieces.

So where did the popular phrase "Kiss my grits!" originate? It all started on the 1970s' sitcom "Alice" where waitress Flo, played by Polly Holliday, routinely uttered her unusual and rather suggestive "Kiss my grits!" to her boss Mel. The expression caught on in the South, where gift shops sold t-shirts, mugs, and other paraphernalia printed with the popular phrase.

Asparagus-Grits Strata

Cubes of cooked grits replace bread in this delicious brunch casserole. Cover the casserole during the last few minutes of cooking to keep the asparagus from drying out while the mixture sets.

3   cups water
1   cup uncooked stone-ground speckled, yellow, or white grits
1   teaspoon salt
1   tablespoon butter
1   cup (4 ounces) grated Asiago cheese, divided
¼   teaspoon black pepper
1   pound asparagus, trimmed and cut into 1¼-inch pieces

2   tablespoons olive oil, divided
1   (8-ounce) package sliced fresh mushrooms
¼   cup dry white wine
Cooking spray
5   large eggs, lightly beaten
1¼ cups half-and-half
1   tablespoon chopped fresh tarragon
½   teaspoon salt
¼   teaspoon black pepper

Combine water, grits, and 1 teaspoon salt in a medium, heavy saucepan; bring to a boil, stirring constantly. Reduce heat; simmer, uncovered, 20 to 25 minutes or until very thick, stirring often. Remove from heat; add butter, ¾ cup cheese, and ¼ teaspoon pepper, stirring until cheese melts. Spoon into a 9-inch square baking pan lined with heavy-duty plastic wrap, spreading evenly; cool 15 minutes. Cover and chill 1 hour or until firm.

Sauté asparagus in 1 tablespoon hot oil in a large skillet over medium-high heat 2 to 3 minutes or until crisp-tender. Remove asparagus from skillet. Sauté mushrooms in remaining 1 tablespoon oil in skillet 3 minutes or until tender. Add wine, and cook until liquid evaporates. Preheat oven to 350°.

Turn chilled grits out onto a cutting board; remove plastic wrap, and cut grits into 1-inch cubes. Place half of asparagus in a 2½-quart baking dish coated with cooking spray; layer with half of grits cubes, half of mushrooms, and remaining grits cubes, mushrooms, and asparagus. Combine eggs, half-and-half, tarragon, ½ teaspoon salt, and ¼ teaspoon pepper; pour egg mixture over asparagus. Sprinkle with remaining ¼ cup cheese. Bake, uncovered, at 350° for 45 minutes to 1 hour or until mixture is set. Cover dish with aluminum foil during last few minutes of baking to prevent asparagus from overcooking. Let stand 10 minutes before serving. **Yield:** 6 to 8 servings.

Egg and Grits Breakfast Cup

Here's proof that you just can't prepare too many grits. This quick morning breakfast uses leftover grits. Just spoon the grits into a custard cup or ramekin, top with an egg, and bake. It's kid-friendly, too—especially if you use blue grits!

save the grits

Rather than toss the leftover cooked grits, refrigerate or freeze them for another meal. Yes, they become very firm and rather gelatinous after chilling, but cold grits can be revived. Just reheat the grits with a little added milk or water, stirring briskly with a whisk or using a potato masher to blend in the additional liquid. My favorite way to recycle leftover grits is with Ham and Grits Quiche on page 35. For a light supper, use grits that were left over from breakfast for the Grits Frittata with Herbs and Shallots on page 37.

½ cup cooked stone-ground grits (plain, buttered, or cheesy)
Cooking spray
1 large egg
Salt to taste
Black pepper to taste
2 tablespoons crumbled cooked sausage or shredded Cheddar cheese or both

Preheat oven to 400°. Spoon cooked grits into a 6-ounce custard cup or ramekin coated with cooking spray. Make a well in center of grits, pressing with fingertips or the back of a spoon and pushing grits up the sides of cup.

Gently break egg into center of grits cup; sprinkle with salt and pepper to taste. Sprinkle with sausage, and place cup in a baking pan; bake at 400° for 22 minutes or until egg is desired degree of doneness. (If adding cheese, bake egg and grits cup 20 minutes; top with cheese, and bake 2 to 4 more minutes or until desired degree of doneness.) **Yield:** 1 serving.

Ham and Grits Quiche

Use your favorite pastry recipe in this tasty grits-filled quiche—another dish that starts with leftover cooked grits. A commercial refrigerated pastry is great to have on hand when you're short on prep time.

Pastry for a 9-inch pie
1 cup cooked stone-ground grits
1 cup (about 5 ounces) chopped cooked ham
1 cup (4 ounces) shredded sharp Cheddar cheese
3 large eggs, lightly beaten
¾ cup half-and-half
1 tablespoon chopped fresh parsley
¼ teaspoon salt
¼ teaspoon black pepper
⅛ teaspoon garlic powder

Preheat oven to 400°. Fit pastry into a 9-inch pie plate; fold edges under and crimp. Prick bottom and sides of piecrust with a fork. Bake at 400° for 8 minutes. Remove from oven; reduce oven temperature to 325°.

Combine cooked grits and next 8 ingredients in a bowl; stir to mix. Spoon mixture into piecrust; bake at 325° for 45 minutes or until set. Let stand 10 minutes before serving. **Yield:** 6 servings.

fresh free-range eggs

The free-range chickens at my father's farm are lucky creatures. Instead of being caged, they roam across horse pastures, nibbling on grass and insects throughout the day. If the chickens are still hungry, they eat organic feed—no antibiotics or hormones for these chicks. As a result, the happy, healthy hens lay eggs with yolks that are darker yellow and more flavorful than most eggs sold in the supermarket.

Grits Frittata with Herbs and Shallots

1   cup water
¼   teaspoon salt
¼   cup uncooked stone-ground yellow
    or white grits
2   ounces cream cheese, softened
1   tablespoon chopped fresh basil
1   tablespoon chopped fresh parsley
2   shallots, thinly sliced and separated
    into rings

1   tablespoon olive oil
4   large eggs, lightly beaten
⅓   cup sliced bottled roasted red bell
    peppers
2   tablespoons grated fresh Asiago or
    Parmesan cheese

If you have leftover grits from an earlier meal, this frittata will be especially quick and easy. Just measure ¾ cup cooked grits into a bowl, and microwave a minute or so to heat through. Add the cream cheese, basil, and parsley to the heated grits, and proceed as directed.

Bring water and salt to a boil in a small, heavy saucepan. Gradually whisk in grits. Cover, reduce heat, and simmer 20 to 25 minutes or until thick, stirring often. (When cooking this small amount of grits, cover pan to avoid losing too much liquid as steam during cooking.) Remove grits from heat. Stir in cream cheese, basil, and parsley; set aside.

Preheat oven to 450°. Sauté shallots in hot oil in a 10-inch ovenproof nonstick skillet over medium heat 5 minutes or just until shallots start to brown.

Whisk eggs into grits mixture; pour grits mixture over shallots in skillet. Carefully place roasted red bell pepper strips on surface of frittata. Cook over low heat, without stirring, 7 to 9 minutes. Sprinkle grated cheese over frittata.

Bake frittata, uncovered, at 450° for 4 to 5 minutes or until set. Let stand 5 minutes. Run a knife around outside edge of skillet, and slide frittata onto a serving plate; cut into wedges to serve. Serve warm or at room temperature.
Yield: 4 servings.

Eggs Florentine with Mornay Sauce

Poach eggs ahead of time, even the night before, to make morning prep easier. Follow the poaching directions shown on the following page, being especially careful not to overcook the eggs. After removing the eggs from the pan, place in ice water to quick chill them, and refrigerate overnight. Just before serving time, drop the eggs into simmering water to heat for about 45 seconds; remove, drain, and serve the reheated eggs immediately.

2¾ cups water
¾ cup uncooked stone-ground grits
¾ teaspoon salt
1   tablespoon butter
6   ounces fresh baby spinach,
    chopped

¼   cup plus 2 tablespoons shredded
    Parmesan cheese
1   large egg, lightly beaten
Cooking spray
4   large fresh eggs, poached
Mornay Sauce

Combine water, grits, and salt in a medium, heavy saucepan; bring to a boil over high heat, stirring constantly. Reduce heat; simmer, uncovered, 20 to 25 minutes or until very thick, stirring often.

Preheat oven to 350°. While grits are cooking, melt butter in a large skillet over medium heat; add spinach, and sauté until spinach wilts and most of the liquid evaporates. Add spinach and Parmesan cheese to hot grits mixture; gradually add 1 beaten egg, stirring to blend. Pour mixture into an 8-inch square baking dish coated with cooking spray. Bake, uncovered, at 350° for 25 minutes or until firm. Remove from oven, and let stand 5 to 10 minutes.

Cut grits mixture into 4 squares; carefully transfer to individual serving plates. Top each with a poached egg and Mornay Sauce. **Yield:** 4 servings.

Mornay Sauce

1   tablespoon butter
1½ tablespoons all-purpose flour
1   cup milk

½   cup (2 ounces) shredded Gruyère
    cheese
⅛   teaspoon salt

Melt butter in a small, heavy saucepan over low heat. Gradually whisk in flour. Cook 1 minute, stirring constantly. Gradually add milk; increase heat to medium, and cook until sauce is thick and bubbly, stirring constantly. Remove from heat, and add cheese and salt, stirring until cheese melts. **Yield:** about 1⅓ cups.

how to poach an egg

Poached eggs are used in many classic brunch dishes, but they can be quite tricky to prepare. You'll get the best results from very fresh eggs. (The whites of older eggs are more likely to disperse into the cooking water.) Follow these steps for poaching success:

Heat water (about 2 inches deep) in a large skillet or saucepan to 160° to 180°. Add 1 tablespoon white vinegar to the water to help set the egg white.

Break each egg into a heat-resistant measuring cup or custard cup. Gently transfer eggs, 1 at a time, into hot water, holding the cup as close as possible to the surface of the water. An easy way to keep the eggs intact during poaching is to drop each egg into a poaching ring or 3-inch jar ring coated with cooking spray (photo 1). Keep the poaching liquid just below a simmer, as boiling will cause the egg white to break apart.

Cook eggs 4 to 8 minutes or until desired degree of doneness (photo 2). Cooking time is affected by the number of eggs cooked at one time—fewer eggs cook more quickly. Lift the poached egg from the water with a slotted spoon, and drain on a paper towel.

Poaching cups make poaching eggs especially easy—just coat the inside of the cups with cooking spray before starting. Break eggs into cups, and place the cups in simmering water in a large skillet. Cover the pan, and cook about 8 minutes. Be sure to keep water at a simmer when using poaching cups.

photo 1

photo 2

sherry vinaigrette:

Chef Stitt considers a perfectly blended vinaigrette one of the most versatile of salad dressings. For Sherry Vinaigrette, he places the leaves from 4 fresh thyme sprigs in a bowl, and adds ½ shallot (finely minced), a good pinch of kosher salt, a good pinch of freshly ground black pepper, and 2 tablespoons sherry vinegar. He lets the mixture macerate (soak) for 10 minutes, and then whisks in 6 tablespoons extra virgin olive oil.

McEwen & Sons Grits with Poached Eggs and Country Ham

Frank Stitt, Chef & Owner, Highlands Bar and Grill, Bottega, and Chez Fonfon, Birmingham, Alabama

4 cups filtered or spring water	¼ cup julienned country ham
½ tablespoon kosher salt	¼ cup port wine
1 cup uncooked stone-ground white grits	½ cup chicken stock
½ cup grated grana padano or Parmigiano-Reggiano cheese	4 large fresh eggs, poached (see page 39)
2 tablespoons butter	1 bunch frisée or watercress, cleaned and dried
Freshly ground black pepper to taste	2 tablespoons Sherry Vinaigrette (at left)
Tabasco to taste	Additional kosher salt and freshly ground black pepper
2 cups button mushrooms, quartered	
1 tablespoon oil	
1 shallot, finely minced	

Combine water and ½ tablespoon kosher salt in a medium, heavy saucepan; bring to a boil. Whisk in grits, and lower heat to a simmer. Cook 20 minutes or until almost tender, stirring occasionally. Remove from heat, and add cheese, butter, pepper to taste (about ⅛ teaspoon), and Tabasco to taste (about ⅛ teaspoon), whisking to combine thoroughly. Cover and keep warm.

Sauté mushrooms in hot oil in a sauté pan or large skillet over medium-high heat about 3 minutes. Add shallot and country ham, and cook 30 seconds. Add port wine and chicken stock, and cook until mixture is reduced by three-fourths.

Spoon grits onto serving plates, and top with poached eggs. Spoon ham and mushroom sauce evenly over the eggs. Toss frisée with vinaigrette, and season with salt and pepper; scatter frisée mixture along the edges of the grits, and serve. **Yield:** 4 servings.

Huevos Rancheros on Cilantro-Grits Cakes

3¼ cups water
1 cup uncooked stone-ground grits
1¼ teaspoons salt
⅓ cup finely chopped onion
1 tablespoon olive oil
1 cup (4 ounces) shredded Monterey Jack cheese
½ cup minced fresh cilantro
Cooking spray

1 cup chopped green bell pepper
1 tablespoon olive oil
1 tablespoon all-purpose flour
1 (8-ounce) can tomato sauce
1 (14.5-ounce) can diced tomatoes with zesty mild green chiles
½ cup rinsed, drained black beans
4 large eggs
Freshly ground black pepper

Poach eggs in a zesty tomato sauce instead of water for this Southwestern brunch favorite. I've modified the original recipe to serve the eggs and sauce over cheesy, cilantro-flavored grits instead of tortillas.

Combine water, grits, and salt in a medium, heavy saucepan; bring to a boil over high heat, stirring constantly. Reduce heat; simmer, uncovered, 20 to 25 minutes or until very thick, stirring often. Meanwhile, sauté onion in 1 tablespoon hot oil in a skillet over medium-high heat 4 minutes or until tender. Add onion, cheese, and cilantro to grits, stirring until cheese melts. Spoon into an 8-inch square baking pan lined with heavy-duty plastic wrap or coated with cooking spray, spreading evenly; cool 15 minutes. Place a dry paper towel over grits; cover and chill 2 hours or until very firm.

Preheat broiler. Turn grits out onto a cutting board; remove plastic wrap, and cut grits into 4 squares. Place squares on a broiler pan coated with cooking spray; coat tops of grits cakes with cooking spray. Broil 5½ inches from heat 5 minutes; flip and broil 7 minutes or until lightly browned.

While grits cakes are broiling, sauté bell pepper in 1 tablespoon hot oil in a skillet 5 minutes. Gradually whisk in flour. Cook 1 minute, stirring constantly. Stir in tomato sauce and tomatoes; simmer 5 minutes. Add beans; bring mixture to a gentle simmer. Break eggs, 1 at a time, into a small, heat-resistant measuring cup; carefully slip eggs, 1 at a time, into tomato mixture in skillet. Cover and cook just below a simmer 8 minutes or until eggs are desired degree of doneness. Place each grits cake on a serving plate; top each with about ¾ cup sauce and 1 egg, and sprinkle with pepper. **Yield:** 4 servings.

Spinach Soufflé-Stuffed Grits Roll

This is a great make-ahead recipe to bake the night before a special brunch. Prepare as directed; after filling and rolling the grits roll, let it cool to room temperature. Cover and chill overnight. Slice the roll into 1¼-inch slices, and place slices on a baking sheet coated with cooking spray. Bake at 350° for 15 to 20 minutes or until thoroughly heated.

4   large eggs
3¾ cups water
1   teaspoon salt
1   cup uncooked stone-ground yellow grits
Cooking spray

1½ cups (6 ounces) shredded part-skim mozzarella cheese
¼   cup half-and-half
⅓   cup shredded Parmesan cheese
2   (12-ounce) packages frozen spinach soufflé (such as Stouffer's)

Separate eggs, and let whites come to room temperature; refrigerate yolks.

Bring water and salt to a boil in a medium, heavy saucepan; gradually whisk in grits. Reduce heat; simmer, uncovered, 20 to 25 minutes or until very thick, stirring often. While grits are cooking, preheat oven to 350°. Coat a 15- x 10-inch jelly-roll pan with cooking spray (this will help hold parchment in place). Line pan with parchment paper, and coat paper with cooking spray.

When grits are done, remove from heat. Add mozzarella cheese and half-and-half to hot grits, stirring to melt cheese. (Grits and cheese mixture will be stringy.) Lightly beat egg yolks, and stir into grits mixture.

Beat egg whites at medium-high speed with an electric mixer until stiff peaks form; gently fold egg whites into grits mixture. Spread grits mixture evenly in prepared jelly-roll pan. Sprinkle with shredded Parmesan cheese. Bake at 350° for 28 to 30 minutes or until top is lightly browned and springs back when lightly touched.

While grits mixture is baking, prepare spinach soufflés in microwave according to package directions. Set aside, and keep warm. Remove baked grits mixture from oven, and turn out onto a second piece of parchment paper that is just a bit larger than pan. Spread hot spinach soufflé mixture over grits roll, leaving a 1-inch border around edges. Gently roll the grits, jelly-roll fashion, beginning on long side, and using parchment to help flip it onto a platter. Slice the roll crosswise into 12 slices, and serve immediately. **Yield:** 6 (2-slice) servings.

We all want to pull out our favorite recipes when it's time for a party. Now you can include the South's favorite grain in appetizers made from stone-ground grits, cornmeal, and polenta. Colorful Grits Bruschetta with Tomato Salsa look pretty on a party platter, while

appetizers

Gruyère Grits Croutons provide amazing crunch atop French Onion Soup. For an eye-catching plated appetizer, be sure to try the crispy Fried Green Tomato Stack with Fig Sauce featuring a stone-ground cornmeal crust.

snackin' good grits

Let these recipes for Gruyère Grits Croutons and Italian-Seasoned Polenta Croutons inspire you to create your own snacks with cooked grits or polenta and your favorite herbs and seasonings. On page 136, you'll find another version of grits croutons that I use to create a Thanksgiving Day-style grits dressing. The secret to getting the grits squares to hold together while cooking is to combine the grits and water in a saucepan and bring to a boil, stirring constantly. This procedure results in cooked grits that are starchier and stick together better than when uncooked grits are added to boiling water and then cooked. (If using polenta for the croutons, add the uncooked polenta to boiling water as usual.) It's also important to cook the grits or polenta the recommended time, even though they will thicken earlier.

French Onion Soup with Gruyère Grits Croutons

pictured on page 46

Gruyère Grits Croutons add a flavorful crunch atop soups such as this French Onion Soup, which is traditionally topped with cheesy bread. A word of warning: You may need to double the recipe for the croutons—they're so addictive and snack-worthy, you may find they've been eaten by kitchen visitors before the soup is ready. If you double the crouton recipe, use a 13- x 9-inch baking pan. Be sure to cook and chill the grits for the croutons ahead of time, so they'll be very firm before baking. For another version of croutons, try Italian-Seasoned Polenta Croutons (opposite page), especially if you're serving minestrone.

1 leek	1 (10½-ounce) can beef consommé
¼ cup butter	1½ teaspoons dried thyme
2 large sweet (Vidalia) onions, peeled and thinly sliced (about 5 cups)	½ teaspoon freshly ground black pepper
2 garlic cloves, minced	1 bay leaf
½ cup dry sherry	Gruyère Grits Croutons
3 cups less-sodium beef broth	

Cut leek in half lengthwise; wash thoroughly (leeks tend to hold sand). Cut leek halves crosswise into thin slices to measure about 1½ cups.

Melt butter in a Dutch oven; add 1½ cups leek, onions, and garlic. Cook, uncovered, over medium-low heat 45 minutes or until onion is very tender and starts to caramelize. Add sherry to onion mixture, and increase heat to medium-high; cook 2 to 3 minutes or until most of liquid evaporates. Stir in beef broth, consommé, thyme, pepper, and bay leaf. Bring to a boil, and cook until thoroughly heated; remove and discard bay leaf. To serve, ladle soup into bowls; top with Gruyère Grits Croutons, and serve immediately. **Yield:** 5 cups.

Gruyère Grits Croutons

3¼ cups less-sodium chicken broth
1 cup uncooked stone-ground yellow
  or white grits
¼ teaspoon salt
1 teaspoon butter

1 cup (4 ounces) shredded Gruyère
  cheese
¼ cup (1 ounce) freshly grated
  Parmesan cheese
Cooking spray

Combine broth, grits, and salt in a medium, heavy saucepan; bring to a boil, stirring constantly. Reduce heat; simmer, uncovered, 20 to 25 minutes or until very thick, stirring often. Remove from heat, and stir in butter and cheeses, stirring to melt.

Spoon mixture into an 8-inch square pan lined with heavy-duty plastic wrap, spreading evenly. Let stand 15 minutes. Place a dry paper towel over grits; cover pan, and chill 1 hour or until very firm.

Preheat oven to 425°. Turn chilled grits out onto a cutting board; remove plastic wrap, and cut grits into 1-inch squares. Place grits squares on a baking sheet coated with cooking spray. Bake at 425° for 20 minutes; flip croutons, and bake 12 more minutes or until lightly browned. **Yield:** about 5 dozen.

Italian-seasoned polenta croutons:

Bring 4 cups water and 1¼ teaspoons salt to a boil in a large, heavy saucepan. Gradually whisk in 1⅓ cups uncooked stone-ground polenta. Reduce heat; simmer, uncovered, 14 minutes or until very thick, stirring often. Remove from heat, and stir in ¼ cup freshly grated pecorino Romano (or Parmesan) cheese, 2 tablespoons minced fresh parsley, 2 tablespoons minced fresh basil, and ¼ teaspoon garlic powder.

Spoon polenta mixture into a 9-inch square pan lined with heavy-duty plastic wrap; let cool. Cover and chill until very firm. Turn chilled polenta out onto a cutting board; remove plastic wrap, and cut into 1¼-inch squares. Pour vegetable oil to a depth of 1½ inches in a large cast-iron skillet; heat to 375°. Dredge polenta squares in all-purpose flour; fry squares, in batches, 3 minutes or until golden brown. Drain on paper towels. Yield: about 4 dozen.

Note: To bake the polenta squares, omit dredging in flour, and simply place the squares on a baking sheet coated with cooking spray. Bake at 425° for 20 minutes; flip squares, and bake 15 more minutes or until lightly browned.

Grits Bruschetta with Tomato Salsa

The colorful salsa that tops this savory bruschetta is best with fresh basil and ripe summer tomatoes. During the winter, substitute a cup of chopped plum tomatoes or grape tomatoes instead. Avoid using the large red tomatoes from the grocery store since they usually have little flavor during the winter months. For another colorful appetizer (winter or summer), top the bruschetta with the Bean and Mango Salsa on page 119. The bruschetta rounds are equally delicious when made with polenta—just adjust the cooking times as described in this recipe.

3 cups water
1 cup uncooked stone-ground white or yellow grits or polenta
1 teaspoon salt
¼ cup (1 ounce) shredded Parmesan cheese
¼ teaspoon garlic powder
¼ teaspoon black pepper
Cooking spray
2 tablespoons extra virgin olive oil, divided
Tomato Salsa

Combine water, grits, and salt in a medium, heavy saucepan; bring to a boil, stirring constantly. Reduce heat; simmer, uncovered, 20 to 25 minutes or until grits are very thick, stirring often. (If using polenta, add polenta to boiling water, reduce heat to medium-low, and cook 14 minutes or until very thick.) Remove grits from heat, and stir in Parmesan cheese, garlic powder, and pepper; pour out onto a flat, heat-resistant surface or baking sheet. Spread to about ⅜-inch thickness (10-inch square); allow to cool completely (about 1 hour) so that the mixture is firm to the touch.

Preheat oven to 350°. Once grits are very firm, cut into rounds with a 1½-inch cookie cutter. Place on a baking sheet coated with cooking spray; brush with 1 tablespoon olive oil. Bake at 350° for 15 minutes. Remove from oven; flip rounds over, and brush other sides with remaining 1 tablespoon olive oil. Return to oven, and bake 10 more minutes. Remove and cool completely. Top rounds with salsa, and serve immediately. **Yield:** about 2 dozen.

Tomato Salsa

1 large tomato, finely chopped
¼ cup minced fresh basil
1 teaspoon minced fresh garlic
1 teaspoon fresh lemon juice
1 teaspoon balsamic vinegar
1 teaspoon extra virgin olive oil
¼ teaspoon salt
¼ teaspoon black pepper

Combine all ingredients in a small bowl; cover and let stand 1 hour. Drain before spooning atop bruschetta. **Yield:** about 1 cup.

Mini Grits Quiche Cups

These quiche cups are super-easy to assemble—especially if you have leftover grits in the refrigerator (you'll need about 1 cup).

1⅓ cups water
¼ teaspoon salt
⅓ cup uncooked stone-ground grits
½ cup (about 2 ounces) diced cooked ham

1 large egg, lightly beaten
¼ cup (1 ounce) freshly grated Parmesan cheese
1 tablespoon minced fresh parsley
2 (2.1-ounce) boxes mini phyllo shells

Preheat oven to 350°. Bring water and salt to a boil in a small, heavy saucepan. Gradually whisk in grits. Reduce heat; simmer, uncovered, 20 to 25 minutes or until thick, stirring often.

Remove grits from heat; stir in ham, egg, Parmesan cheese, and parsley. Place phyllo shells on a baking sheet; spoon about 2 teaspoons grits mixture into each shell. Bake at 350° for 12 minutes. **Yield:** 30 appetizers.

Cheddar-Pecan Crackers

I like to bake a batch of these savory crackers to serve with soup or salad or to have as an afternoon snack. The cornmeal helps the crackers stay crispy for days—just store them in an airtight container.

1 large egg, lightly beaten
1 tablespoon water
½ cup all-purpose flour
½ cup finely ground or sifted stone-ground yellow or white cornmeal (see page 23)
¼ teaspoon baking powder

¼ teaspoon salt
¼ teaspoon ground red pepper
¼ cup cold butter, cut into small pieces
½ cup (2 ounces) shredded extra sharp Cheddar cheese
½ cup finely chopped pecans
3 to 4 tablespoons cold water

Preheat oven to 375°. Combine egg and 1 tablespoon water, stirring until blended; set aside.

Combine flour and next 4 ingredients in a bowl until well blended; add butter, and cut in with a pastry blender or fingertips until mixture is crumbly. Stir in cheese and pecans. Add 3 to 4 tablespoons cold water, and toss gently with a fork until mixture is moistened and forms a ball.

Turn dough out onto a lightly floured surface, and shape into a round disk. Roll out dough to about ¼-inch thickness. Cut with a 2-inch biscuit or cookie cutter, and place on a baking sheet lined with parchment paper. Brush dough lightly with egg wash. Bake at 375° for 15 minutes or until lightly browned. Transfer crackers to a wire rack to cool completely. Store crackers in an airtight container. **Yield:** about 2 dozen.

Fried Green Tomato Stack with Fig Sauce

This recipe features a Southern favorite, cornmeal-crusted fried green tomatoes.
The combination of smooth fresh mozzarella with tangy tomatoes and crispy
pancetta, all drizzled with a sweet fig glaze, makes for a delightful culinary treat.

4   thin slices pancetta (about 1.2 ounces)
¼   cup all-purpose flour
½   cup stone-ground yellow or white cornmeal
½   teaspoon kosher salt
1   large egg, lightly beaten
1   tablespoon water
1   green tomato, cut into 4 (½-inch-thick) slices

Peanut oil for frying
4   slices fresh mozzarella cheese (about 4 ounces)
⅓   cup fig preserves
1   tablespoon honey
1   teaspoon balsamic vinegar
1   teaspoon sugar
1   fresh or dried fig, cut into wedges
Additional honey (optional)

Preheat oven to 400°. Line a 15- x 10-inch jelly-roll pan with aluminum foil. Place pancetta slices on foil-lined pan, and bake at 400° for 6 to 8 minutes or until pancetta is fully cooked. Crumble pancetta, and set aside.

Place flour in a shallow dish; combine cornmeal and salt in a second shallow dish. Combine egg and water in a third shallow dish. Lightly dredge tomato slices in flour. Dip in egg mixture, and coat in cornmeal mixture. Pour oil to a depth of ¼ to ½ inch in a large cast-iron skillet; heat over medium-high heat until hot. Place tomato slices in hot oil, and cook 2 minutes on each side or until golden brown. Remove tomato slices to a wire rack placed over a layer of paper towels; place mozzarella slices on top of hot tomato slices.

Combine fig preserves, 1 tablespoon honey, balsamic vinegar, and sugar in a small saucepan. Cook over medium-high heat 5 minutes or until mixture has thinned slightly. Remove from heat, and drizzle 1 tablespoon fig sauce over mozzarella on each tomato slice. Top each with crumbled pancetta, and drizzle with remaining fig sauce. Garnish with fig wedges, and drizzle with additional honey, if desired. **Yield:** 4 appetizer servings.

fresh figs

Fig trees thrive in the warm climate of the southern United States—although Californians may argue that their climate produces the best figs in the country. Like many Southerners, I have fond memories of my parents' fig trees loaded with plump, ripe figs during the late summer. Even small children could pluck the juicy fruit from the low-hanging limbs. Each summer Mother prepared big batches of fig preserves to "put up" for the winter in tall, quart-sized canning jars. She could never add too much sugar to the preserves to satisfy Daddy's sweet tooth! Throughout the winter, we'd enjoy the syrupy, sweet preserves on hot buttered biscuits for breakfast almost every morning.

Stone-Ground Grits and Portobello

Nick Heinrich, Chef, Crooked Porch Bar B Que, Napa, California

Nick Heinrich, Chef, Crooked Porch Bar B Que, Napa, California

chef's recipe

Chef Heinrich has taken Southern-style grits to the wine country, and one of his most requested appetizers is this combination of grilled Portobellos over rich, cream-laden grits drizzled with a delicious Bordelaise sauce. Like many chefs, Nick keeps a pot of veal stock simmering on the stovetop and prepares Bordelaise sauce by the gallon. If you'd like to make an adaptation of his Bordelaise Sauce (in a smaller quantity), you may be able to purchase veal stock at a specialty food store or you can substitute commercial beef stock instead. The commercial stock or broth results in a less-viscous sauce, so I recommend thickening the Bordelaise with a slurry of 3 tablespoons cornstarch and 3 tablespoons broth or water.

2 tablespoons unsalted butter (Nick uses European-style butter)	2 cups uncooked stone-ground yellow grits
1½ tablespoons chopped fresh shallots	¼ cup (1 ounce) freshly grated Parmigiano-Reggiano cheese
½ tablespoon chopped fresh garlic	2 splashes of Tabasco sauce
½ teaspoon chopped fresh thyme	Bordelaise Sauce
1 quart heavy whipping cream	4 large Portobello mushroom caps
1 quart water	3 tablespoons olive oil
Kosher salt to taste	2 teaspoons chopped fresh thyme
Black pepper to taste	

Melt butter in a medium, heavy saucepan; add shallots, garlic, and ½ teaspoon thyme. Sauté over medium heat 3 to 4 minutes or until garlic and shallots are soft but not browned. Add cream, water, kosher salt to taste (about 4 teaspoons), and pepper to taste (about ¼ teaspoon) to shallot mixture; cook over medium-high heat just until mixture starts to boil. Gradually whisk grits into cream mixture. Reduce heat to low, and cook, uncovered, 40 minutes, stirring often. Remove from heat, and stir in Parmigiano-Reggiano cheese and Tabasco sauce; cover and keep warm.

Prepare Bordelaise Sauce, and keep warm.

While grits are cooking, remove stems and gills from mushroom caps; clean mushroom caps. Brush with olive oil, sprinkle with 2 teaspoons chopped fresh thyme, and season with additional kosher salt and black pepper. Let stand 5 minutes.

Preheat grill to 300° to 350° (medium). Grill mushrooms, covered with grill lid, about 4 minutes on each side. Remove from grill, and let rest 2 minutes. Slice each mushroom into 6 pieces. Serve mushrooms and Bordelaise Sauce over grits. **Yield:** 8 hearty appetizer servings.

Bordelaise Sauce

1	tablespoon olive oil	2	bay leaves
2	carrots, chopped	2	quarts veal stock or commercial beef stock
½	cup finely chopped shallots	2	ounces beef bone marrow (from about 4 [2-inch] shank bones), diced and rinsed (or substitute 4 tablespoons unsalted butter)
2	garlic cloves, minced		
1½	cups dry red wine		
½	bunch fresh flat-leaf Italian parsley		
2	sprigs fresh thyme		Kosher salt to taste
½	tablespoon black peppercorns		

Heat olive oil in a sauté pan or large skillet; add carrots, and cook over medium-low heat 7 to 8 minutes or until carrots are very tender and starting to caramelize. Add shallots and garlic, and cook 6 to 8 minutes or until transparent. Add wine, and bring to a boil. Cook over high heat about 5 minutes to deglaze pan (stirring to loosen particles from bottom of skillet). Add parsley, thyme, peppercorns, and bay leaves; cook 5 to 10 more minutes or until mixture is thick and "syrupy." Add veal stock and marrow; bring to a boil, and cook 30 minutes or until mixture coats the back of a wooden spoon. Season to taste with kosher salt (about 1 teaspoon). Strain twice through a fine strainer. **Yield:** about 4 cups.

chef's secret: bone marrow

Bordelaise sauce traditionally calls for finishing the sauce with bone marrow, an ingredient not often found in most home kitchens. To obtain marrow, purchase cross-cut shank bones from your local meat market. Run a small sharp knife around the inside edge of the bone to separate the marrow; then push the marrow out with a finger. Rinse, dice, and refrigerate the marrow or use as directed. If you'd prefer not to use bone marrow, you can substitute unsalted butter for a similar result.

Just as cooks in other parts of the country depend on wheat flour for breadmaking, Southerners have traditionally looked to cornmeal for our daily sustenance in the form of cornbread, cornsticks, hush puppies, and hoecakes. Turn the page for a

breads

dependable old-fashioned cornbread recipe along with what has become my new favorite: brightly colored blue and yellow Marbled Cornbread. You'll also find cornmeal-enriched scones, waffles, pancakes, yeast rolls, and foccacia.

Southern favorite

Old-Fashioned Buttermilk Cornbread

for an 8-inch skillet

This recipe illus̶t̶ ̶ ̶s the many ways that Southern cooks prepare cornbread. First, there's the color—yellow or white? Some like it with sugar, and for others the slightest sweet taste is just wrong. Many prefer to make their cornbread with bacon grease instead of oil, but others, like myself, can't see loading an otherwise very healthy bread with what nutritionists consider a rather unhealthy fat. Buttermilk adds an interesting tanginess, but when there's no buttermilk in the refrigerator, I make my cornbread with nonfat milk.

2 teaspoons vegetable oil or shortening
1 cup stone-ground white or yellow cornmeal
1½ teaspoons sugar (optional)
1 teaspoon baking powder
½ teaspoon salt
⅔ cup buttermilk, whole milk, or nonfat milk
2 tablespoons melted butter, vegetable oil, or bacon grease
1 large egg, lightly beaten

Grease an 8-inch cast-iron skillet with 2 teaspoons oil or shortening; place in oven. Preheat oven to 425°. (If oven is already preheated, place pan in hot oven for 5 minutes or until hot.)

Combine cornmeal, sugar, if desired, baking powder, and salt in a bowl until well blended. Add buttermilk, butter, and egg, stirring just until dry ingredients are moistened. Swirl hot oil in preheated skillet to coat; pour batter into skillet. Bake at 425° for 18 minutes or until lightly browned.
Yield: 4 servings.

cast-iron rules

To season a new cast-iron skillet (or to reseason a skillet that smells metallic or has developed a dull gray color), scrub it first with hot soapy water and a stiff brush. After rinsing and drying it thoroughly, spread a thin layer of vegetable oil or melted shortening on both the inside and outside of the skillet. Place a piece of aluminum foil on the bottom rack of the oven to catch drips, and preheat the oven to 300°. Place the skillet upside down on the top rack of the oven, and bake for at least an hour. Turn the oven off, and let the skillet cool in the oven with the door closed. Once the skillet is seasoned, you should avoid washing it with soap; instead just clean it with a brush and hot water. After towel drying, you can rub on a thin layer of oil while the skillet is still warm.

Old-Fashioned Buttermilk Cornbread

for a 10-inch skillet

Prepare recipe as directed for an 8-inch skillet (opposite page), using twice the amount listed for each ingredient. Pour batter into a greased and preheated 10-inch cast-iron skillet, and bake at 425° for 22 to 24 minutes or until lightly browned. **Yield:** 8 servings.

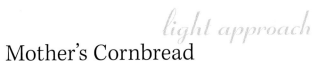

light approach

Mother's Cornbread

Always looking for ways to cook healthy meals, Mother has always made her pones of cornbread without a drop of fat. And like many Southerners, she and Daddy prefer very crusty cornbread, which she creates by omitting the egg and baking the cornmeal batter in the larger 10-inch skillet.

1 cup stone-ground yellow or white cornmeal	¾ teaspoon salt
½ cup all-purpose flour	1¼ to 1⅓ cups nonfat buttermilk
1½ teaspoons baking powder	1 large egg (optional)
¼ teaspoon baking soda	Cooking spray
	Additional stone-ground cornmeal

Preheat oven to 425°. Combine first 5 ingredients in a bowl until well blended. Combine 1¼ cups buttermilk and, if desired, egg; add to cornmeal mixture, adding additional buttermilk as needed to make a pourable batter. (If you omit the egg, use 1⅓ cups buttermilk.)

Coat an 8-inch or 10-inch cast-iron skillet with cooking spray; dust with additional cornmeal. Pour cornmeal mixture into skillet; bake at 425° for 22 to 24 minutes or until lightly browned. **Yield:** 4 to 6 servings.

cornbread and milk

My family, like many Southerners, grew up enjoying vegetable dinners throughout the summer—with fresh vegetables straight from the summer garden. Mother always spooned a type of relish called chow-chow onto her plate, Daddy and my brother, Frank, smeared mayonnaise over their sliced red tomatoes, and my sister, Ann, topped her black-eyed peas with ketchup. But all of us ate "cornbread and milk"—a truly Southern concoction of crumbled pieces of warm cornbread dropped into a glass of cold milk and eaten with a spoon.

Marbled Cornbread

Chris Richardson, Head Baker, The Continental Bakery,
Birmingham, Alabama

For the yellow batter:

1½ cups finely ground stone-ground
   yellow cornmeal
1 cup bread flour
1 tablespoon sugar
1 tablespoon baking powder
½ teaspoon baking soda
¾ teaspoon salt
½ cup butter, melted and cooled
6 tablespoons bacon drippings or
   additional melted butter, cooled
1 large egg
1½ cups buttermilk (see chef's secret
   at right)
Cooking spray

For the blue batter:

1½ cups finely ground stone-ground
   blue cornmeal
1 cup bread flour
1 tablespoon sugar
1 tablespoon baking powder
½ teaspoon baking soda
¾ teaspoon salt
½ cup butter, melted and cooled
6 tablespoons bacon drippings or
   additional melted butter, cooled
1 large egg
1½ cups buttermilk

Place a 10-inch cast-iron skillet in oven; preheat oven to 400°.

For the yellow batter, combine first 6 ingredients in a large bowl until well blended. Repeat procedure with first 6 ingredients for the blue batter in a second large bowl.

Whisk ½ cup cooled melted butter and bacon drippings into each bowl. Add egg to each bowl; stir to blend. Add buttermilk to each bowl; stir to blend.

Remove skillet from oven, and coat with cooking spray. Pour yellow batter into preheated skillet; quickly top with blue batter, and fold the batters together with a rubber spatula to get a marbled look. Place skillet back in oven, and bake at 400° for 25 minutes. Reduce oven temperature to 325°, and bake 15 more minutes. **Yield:** 10 to 12 servings.

chef's recipe

The Continental Bakery's breads and pastries are touted as works of art. They are prepared daily from scratch by artisan bakers who really care about good bread and who rely on traditional European methods. Owned by Carole Griffin, the bakery's attention to detail and use of natural ingredients results in authentic European breads, often with a Southern twist. Chris Richardson, the Head Baker, applies that same kind of artistic approach to traditional Southern cornbread with his beautiful rounds of blue and yellow Marbled Cornbread. According to Chris, "Creativity is suggested to personalize your marbled cornbread. No two should look exactly the same."

chef's secret

Instead of buttermilk, Chris uses 1¼ cups of milk mixed with 4 ounces of white sourdough starter (a common ingredient for bakeries to use). After mixing the two, he places the mixture in the refrigerator for the sourdough starter to soften. He uses a small whisk or fork to break up the starter before adding it to the dry cornmeal mixture in place of the buttermilk. His sourdough version is wonderful, but I absolutely love this buttermilk version as well.

Cracklin' Cornbread

Chris and Idie Hastings, Chefs & Owners, Hot and Hot Fish Club,
Birmingham, Alabama

chef's recipe

Chris and Idie Hastings add a touch of sophistication to the South's favorite bread for their patrons at the upscale Hot and Hot Fish Club. Chris recommends that during the winter when you can't find good fresh corn, you can still prepare this recipe substituting 1 cup frozen thawed corn for the fresh; pulse the corn in a food processor 4 to 5 times before sautéing with the green onions. For dessert, try another of the Hastings' delightful creations, Warm Johnny Cakes with Blackberries (page 165).

2 tablespoons vegetable oil, divided
¼ cup diced thick-cut applewood smoked bacon (about 2 slices)
1 cup freshly shaved yellow corn
½ cup thinly sliced green onions (about 6 small)
1 cup stone-ground yellow cornmeal
⅓ cup corn flour (finely ground cornmeal)
⅓ cup all-purpose flour
1 teaspoon baking powder
1 teaspoon kosher salt
¼ teaspoon freshly ground black pepper
1 large egg, lightly beaten
1½ cups whole buttermilk

Heat ½ tablespoon oil in a medium, heavy skillet over medium-low heat. Add bacon, and cook 5 to 8 minutes or until browned and crispy, stirring occasionally. Add corn and green onions, and sauté 1 minute. Remove skillet from heat, and set aside to cool slightly.

Add remaining 1½ tablespoons oil to an 8-inch cast-iron skillet, and swirl to coat skillet; place skillet in oven. Preheat the oven to 400°.

Combine cornmeal, corn flour, all-purpose flour, baking powder, salt, and pepper in a large bowl; stir with a whisk. Combine egg and buttermilk in a small bowl, stirring with a whisk until blended. Add buttermilk mixture to cornmeal mixture. Stir in bacon and onion mixture, mixing thoroughly.

Remove skillet from oven; pour cornmeal mixture into preheated skillet. Bake at 400° for 22 to 25 minutes or until cooked through and golden brown; serve warm. **Yield:** 6 to 8 servings.

Cornsticks with Jalapeños

pictured on page 58

I've seen cornsticks shaped like cactus and others shaped like fish, but the classic cast-iron pan results in cornsticks shaped like small ears of corn.

Cooking spray

1 tablespoon butter

3 to 4 tablespoons seeded, minced jalapeño pepper (about 1½ peppers)

⅔ cup stone-ground yellow or white cornmeal

¼ cup all-purpose flour

1 teaspoon baking powder

¼ teaspoon salt

½ cup nonfat milk

1 large egg, lightly beaten

Coat a cast-iron cornstick pan with cooking spray, and place in oven. Preheat oven to 425°. (If oven is already preheated, place pan in hot oven for about 5 minutes.)

Melt butter in a small skillet over medium heat; add jalapeño pepper, and sauté 3 minutes or until tender.

Combine cornmeal, flour, baking powder, and salt in a bowl until well blended. Combine milk and egg; add to cornmeal mixture, and stir just until blended. Stir in cooked jalapeños. Spoon mixture into preheated cornstick pan, filling full; bake at 425° for 15 minutes or until lightly browned. **Yield:** 7 cornsticks.

blue cornsticks with onion:
Substitute blue cornmeal for yellow cornmeal, and minced onion for minced jalapeño pepper.

Hot-Water Cornbread Patties

Some folks call this old-fashioned bread "hot-water bread," while others call the crisp patties "hoecakes." Kelly Troiano, my editor, makes my mouth water when she tells about a favorite childhood memory—helping her grandmother fry cornbread patties for weeknight suppers. I love to hear Kelly fondly describe the crisp, lacy edges that formed around the patties while the cornmeal batter sizzled in the hot oil.

history of hoecakes

Southern cornbread has a humble origin—the first recipes combined cornmeal, hog or bear grease, and water or milk. Early cooks dropped this simple batter onto the flat side of a hoe and baked the "hoecakes" over a hot fire.

oven-fried hot-water cornbread patties:

Preheat oven to 450°. Pour ¼ cup vegetable oil in a 15- x 10-inch jelly-roll pan; place in preheated oven for 5 minutes. Prepare batter as directed above. Carefully remove pan from oven, and spoon batter by ¼ cupfuls into hot oil, spreading each to a 3-inch diameter. Bake at 450° for 10 minutes; turn patties over, and bake 8 more minutes or until crisp and brown.

2 cups stone-ground yellow or white cornmeal	¼ cup milk
2 teaspoons sugar (optional)	2 tablespoons vegetable oil
1 teaspoon baking powder	1¼ to 1½ cups boiling water (see Note)
1 teaspoon salt	Additional vegetable oil

Combine cornmeal, sugar, if desired, baking powder, and salt in a bowl until well blended. Stir in milk and 2 tablespoons oil. Gradually add boiling water, stirring until batter is the consistency of pancake batter.

Pour additional vegetable oil to a depth of ½ inch in a large, heavy skillet; place over medium-high heat until hot. Using a ¼-cup measure, drop batter into hot oil; fry, in batches, 3 minutes on each side or until golden brown. Drain on paper towels. **Yield:** 8 patties.

Note: The amount of boiling water needed varies depending on the type of cornmeal used. If the batter is too thick, it won't spread out when it hits the hot oil. If too thin, the batter will spread and the patties will be too thin.

Easy Cornbread Crisps

pictured on page 96

Here's an easy, oven-friendly version of the old-fashioned hoecake that's perfect for serving alongside Turkey Corn Chili (page 96) or your favorite soup.

2	cups stone-ground yellow or white cornmeal	¼	cup butter, melted, or vegetable oil
2	teaspoons sugar	1	large egg, lightly beaten
1	teaspoon baking powder	1¼	cups boiling water
1	teaspoon salt		Cooking spray

Preheat oven to 425°. Combine first 4 ingredients in a large bowl until well blended; stir in butter and egg. Gradually add boiling water, stirring to blend. Spoon rounds of batter (about 2 tablespoons each) onto a baking sheet coated with cooking spray; spread to a 2¼-inch diameter. Bake at 425° for 13 to 15 minutes or until lightly browned on bottom and on edges. **Yield:** 1½ dozen.

Old-Fashioned Hush Puppies

pictured on page 104

Where did the name hush puppy originate? The story I've heard is that early cooks would toss scraps of fried cornmeal batter to their hungry dogs to discourage their begging for food, while commanding the barking dog to "Hush, Puppy!" I feel sure that the other food being cooked was fried fish, because no fish dinner would be complete without hush puppies on the side.

¾	cup stone-ground cornmeal	⅛	teaspoon ground red pepper
¼	cup all-purpose flour	1	large egg, lightly beaten
2	teaspoons sugar	½	cup buttermilk
1	teaspoon baking powder	⅓	cup diced onion
½	teaspoon salt		Vegetable oil

Combine first 6 ingredients in a bowl until well blended; make a well in center of mixture. Combine egg, buttermilk, and onion; add to dry ingredients, stirring just until moistened.

Pour oil to a depth of 2 inches into a Dutch oven; heat to 375°. Drop batter by rounded tablespoons into hot oil. Fry hush puppies in hot oil, in batches, 1 to 2 minutes on each side or until golden brown. (It's best to use a deep-fat thermometer to keep the temperature hot enough but not too hot. Cook the hush puppies in batches to avoid crowding the skillet.) Drain hush puppies on paper towels; serve immediately. **Yield:** about 1½ dozen.

Cornmeal-Banana Bread

Be sure to use very ripe bananas for this tasty bread that's great right out of the oven and is even better the next day.

⅓	cup butter, softened	¼	teaspoon baking powder
½	(8-ounce) package cream cheese, softened	¼	teaspoon baking soda
		¼	teaspoon salt
1	cup sugar	¾	cup mashed ripe bananas (about 2 bananas)
1	large egg		
1	cup all-purpose flour	½	cup chopped pecans
½	cup finely ground or sifted stone-ground cornmeal (see page 23)	1	teaspoon vanilla extract
			Cooking spray

Preheat oven to 350°. Beat butter and cream cheese at medium speed with an electric mixer until creamy. Gradually add sugar, beating until light and fluffy. Add egg, beating just until blended.

Combine flour and next 4 ingredients in a bowl until well blended. Gradually add dry ingredients to butter mixture, beating at low speed just until blended. Stir in bananas, pecans, and vanilla; spoon batter into an 8½- x 4½-inch loaf pan coated with cooking spray.

Bake at 350º for 1 hour or until a wooden pick inserted in center comes out clean and sides pull away from pan. (Shield with aluminum foil during last 15 minutes of baking to prevent overbrowning, if needed.) Cool bread in pan on a wire rack 5 minutes. Remove from pan, and cool 30 minutes before slicing. **Yield:** 1 loaf.

baked hush puppies:
Prepare batter as directed; spoon into 1¾-inch miniature muffin cups coated with cooking spray. Bake at 425° for 12 to 14 minutes or until lightly browned. Yield: 15 hush puppies.

cornmeal-banana muffins:
Prepare batter as directed for Cornmeal-Banana Bread. To bake muffins, spoon batter evenly into 2½-inch muffin cups coated with cooking spray. Bake at 350° for 20 to 25 minutes or until a wooden pick inserted in center comes out clean. Cool in pan 10 minutes. Yield: 1 dozen.

Blueberry Muffins with Streusel Topping

Blue cornmeal contributes color, flavor, and texture to these delightful muffins. Feel free to use yellow or white cornmeal instead.

¼ cup sugar

2½ tablespoons all-purpose flour

¼ teaspoon ground cinnamon

1½ tablespoons butter

1¼ cups all-purpose flour

½ cup finely ground or sifted stone-ground blue, white, or yellow cornmeal (see page 23)

½ cup sugar

1 tablespoon baking powder

¾ teaspoon salt

1 teaspoon grated lemon rind

1 large egg, lightly beaten

¾ cup milk

⅓ cup vegetable oil

1 cup fresh or frozen blueberries

1 tablespoon all-purpose flour

1 tablespoon sugar

Cooking spray

Preheat oven to 400°. Combine ¼ cup sugar, 2½ tablespoons flour, and cinnamon in a bowl; cut in butter with a pastry blender or fingertips until mixture is crumbly. Set aside.

Combine 1¼ cups flour and next 5 ingredients in a medium bowl until well blended; make a well in center of mixture. Combine egg, milk, and oil; add to cornmeal mixture, stirring just until moistened.

Combine blueberries, 1 tablespoon flour, and 1 tablespoon sugar, tossing gently to coat. Fold blueberry mixture into batter. Spoon batter evenly into 10 (2½-inch) muffin cups coated with cooking spray; sprinkle cinnamon mixture over batter. Bake muffins at 400° for 20 minutes or until lightly browned and muffins spring back when touched lightly in center. Remove from pans immediately. **Yield:** 10 muffins.

year-round freshness

Don't limit blueberry muffins to the summer-peak growing season. Buy lots of fresh blueberries (or pick your own!) when they're available. They freeze easily and can be enjoyed throughout the year in muffins, pancakes, and scones. Just place clean, dry berries in a single layer on a large baking pan, and freeze until firm. Transfer the berries to freezer bags, and return to the freezer until you're ready to cook them—you don't even need to thaw them first.

Cinnamon-Raisin Drop Biscuits

Cornmeal adds a slight crunch to these easy breakfast biscuits.

flour with a Southern twist

Cooks in the South love to bake biscuits with the Southern brands of all-purpose or self-rising flour, White Lily and Martha White. These flours are milled from soft red winter wheat and are perfect for producing tender biscuits and cakes. I like to keep a bag of White Lily self-rising flour on hand for a super-quick batch of biscuits for breakfast. If you can't find one of these Southern flours, combine one part all-purpose flour with one part cake flour for similar results. And, if your recipe calls for self-rising flour, you can add 1 teaspoon baking powder and ½ teaspoon salt to 1 cup all-purpose flour.

1 cup soft-wheat self-rising flour (such as White Lily)
½ cup finely ground or sifted stone-ground cornmeal (see page 23)
2 tablespoons granulated sugar
½ teaspoon baking powder
¾ teaspoon ground cinnamon
⅓ cup cold butter, cut into small pieces
½ cup raisins
½ cup milk
Cooking spray
½ cup sifted powdered sugar
2 to 3 teaspoons half-and-half

Preheat oven to 400°. Combine first 5 ingredients in a bowl until well blended; cut in butter with a pastry blender or fingertips until mixture is crumbly. Add raisins, and toss to coat. Add milk, stirring with a fork just until moistened.

Coat a ¼-cup measure with cooking spray, and use measure to scoop dough onto a baking sheet lined with parchment paper. Bake at 400° for 15 minutes or until lightly browned. Combine powdered sugar and half-and-half; drizzle over warm biscuits. **Yield:** 6 biscuits.

Orange-Cranberry Scones

As a variation, try a lemon-glazed blueberry scone, using blue cornmeal instead of white. Omit the orange rind in the dough, and add fresh blueberries instead of cranberries. For the glaze, substitute lemon rind for orange rind and lemon juice for orange juice.

1½ cups all-purpose flour

½ cup finely ground or sifted stone-ground white or yellow cornmeal (see page 23)

⅓ cup granulated sugar

2½ teaspoons baking powder

½ teaspoon salt

1 tablespoon grated orange rind

⅓ cup cold butter, cut into small pieces

½ cup sweetened dried cranberries

1 large egg, lightly beaten

¾ cup heavy whipping cream

Turbinado sugar (optional)

1 cup powdered sugar

1 tablespoon butter, melted

¼ teaspoon grated orange rind

1 tablespoon fresh orange juice

1 to 2 teaspoons heavy whipping cream (if needed)

Preheat oven to 400°. Combine first 6 ingredients in a large bowl until well blended. Add butter, and cut in with a pastry blender or fingertips until mixture is crumbly. Stir in cranberries.

Combine egg and ¾ cup cream; add to dry ingredients, stirring just until blended. Turn dough out onto a lightly floured surface, and roll out to about ¾-inch thickness (about 7½-inch diameter round). Transfer to a parchment paper-lined baking sheet. Use a floured sharp knife to cut dough into 8 wedges. Separate wedges to about ⅜ inch between wedges. Sprinkle with turbinado sugar, if desired. Bake scones at 400° for 18 to 20 minutes or until golden brown.

Combine powdered sugar and next 3 ingredients in a bowl; stir in 1 to 2 teaspoons cream, if needed, to make a thin glaze. Drizzle over warm scones. **Yield:** 8 scones.

Serve these scones alongside the Spinach Soufflé-Stuffed Grits Roll (page 44) for a perfect-for-company weekend brunch.

Cornmeal Griddle Cakes

Nutritionists often proclaim the benefits of eating more fiber, and what better way to accomplish that goal than with delicious, homemade whole-grain bread?

1	cup whole wheat flour	½	teaspoon salt
1	cup finely ground or sifted stone-ground white or yellow cornmeal (see page 23)	1	large egg, lightly beaten
		1	cup milk
¼	cup sugar	½	cup sour cream
½	teaspoon baking powder	¼	cup vegetable oil
1	teaspoon baking soda		Cooking spray
			Honey or maple syrup

Combine first 6 ingredients in a large bowl until well blended. Combine egg, milk, sour cream, and oil in a separate bowl; add to dry ingredients, stirring just until moistened.

Pour about ¼ cup batter for each cake onto a hot griddle coated with cooking spray. Spread batter to about a 4-inch diameter using back of a spoon. Cook 1½ to 2 minutes or until edges start looking dry; turn and cook 1 to 2 more minutes or until desired degree of doneness. Serve cakes warm with honey or maple syrup. **Yield:** about 1 dozen.

Oatmeal Pancakes with Cornmeal and Flaxseed

Frank's wife, Helen, cooks almost everything from scratch, using his freshly ground McEwen & Sons cornmeal, rolled oats, whole wheat flour, and flaxseed. She's even able to cook with the freshest eggs possible, supplied by Frank, Jr. and Luke's chickens, which roam freely on the farm just down the road. Here's one of the boys' favorite breakfast recipes, which in their opinion is always best with fresh blueberries.

flaxseed benefits

In recent years, researchers have found that flaxseed is loaded with essential nutrients, including Omega-3 fatty acids, fiber, and phytochemicals called lignans. As a result, flaxseed may help reduce total cholesterol and LDL ("bad") cholesterol, thereby reducing the risk of heart disease. Because the whole seed is not as digestible as ground flaxseed, it's best to grind the flaxseed before using in a recipe—use a clean coffee grinder to grind the seed easily. Take advantage of the health benefits of flaxseed by mixing a tablespoon or so into yogurt, sprinkling it over cereal, or adding it to pancakes or muffins as in the recipe above.

1   cup uncooked regular oats
½   cup McEwen & Sons finely ground blue, yellow, or white cornmeal
1   tablespoon baking powder
1   teaspoon salt
½   cup freshly ground flaxseed
2   large eggs, lightly beaten
1¼ cups organic 1% low-fat milk
1   cup plain organic yogurt
¼   cup vegetable oil
¼   cup honey
Cooking spray
Fresh blueberries (optional)

Combine first 5 ingredients in a large bowl until well blended; make a well in center of mixture. Combine eggs, milk, yogurt, oil, and honey in a bowl; add to dry ingredients, stirring just until moistened. Let mixture stand 10 minutes.

Pour about ¼ cup batter per pancake onto a hot nonstick griddle or skillet coated with cooking spray; top with a sprinkling of fresh blueberries, if desired. Cook until edges look cooked; carefully turn pancakes over, and cook until bottoms look cooked. (Bubbles don't form on the uncooked tops of the pancakes as with traditional pancake batter.) **Yield:** 20 (4-inch) pancakes.

Whole Wheat–Cornmeal Waffles

1   cup whole wheat flour
1   cup finely ground or sifted stone-ground white or yellow cornmeal (see page 23)
2   tablespoons sugar
½   teaspoon baking powder
1   teaspoon baking soda
½   teaspoon salt
1   large egg, lightly beaten
1   cup milk
½   cup sour cream
3   tablespoons vegetable oil
Cooking spray
Honey or maple syrup

Combine first 6 ingredients in a large bowl until well blended. Combine egg, milk, sour cream, and oil in a separate bowl; add to dry ingredients, stirring just until moistened.

Pour about 1 cup batter onto a preheated 8-inch square waffle iron lightly coated with cooking spray. Cook waffles 2 minutes or until lightly browned. Serve waffles warm with maple syrup or honey. **Yield:** 10 waffles.

Multi-Grain Spoon Rolls

1	(¼-ounce) envelope rapid-rise yeast (2¼ teaspoons)	1	cup bread flour
1½	cups warm water (100° to 110°)	1	cup whole wheat pastry flour
¼	cup butter, melted and cooled	1	cup stone-ground cornmeal
¼	cup sugar	1	tablespoon baking powder
1	large egg	1	teaspoon salt
			Cooking spray

Combine yeast and water in a large mixing bowl, stirring to dissolve; let stand 5 minutes. Stir in butter, sugar, and egg. Combine flours, cornmeal, baking powder, and salt; gradually add to yeast mixture, beating at medium speed with an electric mixer until smooth. Spoon dough into 2½-inch muffin cups coated with cooking spray, filling about three-fourths full. Let rise in a warm place (85°), free from drafts, 30 minutes.

Preheat oven to 375°. Bake rolls at 375° for 18 to 20 minutes or until lightly browned. Remove rolls from pan immediately. **Yield:** 1½ dozen.

Note: Dough may be refrigerated up to 24 hours. Baking time may need to be increased by about 5 minutes.

Be sure to follow your waffle maker's instruction book for the amount of batter and recommended cooking time for each waffle.

Cornmeal Focaccia with Rosemary

When making focaccia, I like to let my heavy-duty electric mixer do the kneading work for me. But you can always knead the dough yourself on a lightly floured countertop or pastry cloth. Some bakers use their fingers to poke holes in the focaccia dough before brushing it with olive oil, which allows more olive oil to penetrate the dough.

1   (¼-ounce) envelope rapid-rise yeast
    (2¼ teaspoons)
1⅔ cups warm water (100° to 110°)
2   tablespoons extra virgin olive oil
1   tablespoon sugar
1¼ teaspoons salt
2   cups bread flour
1   cup whole wheat flour

1   cup finely ground or sifted
    stone-ground white or yellow
    cornmeal (see page 23)
3   tablespoons chopped fresh
    rosemary, divided
Cooking spray
2   to 4 tablespoons extra virgin
    olive oil

Combine yeast and water, stirring to dissolve; let stand 2 to 3 minutes. Whisk together yeast mixture, 2 tablespoons olive oil, sugar, and salt in a mixing bowl. Add flours and cornmeal to yeast mixture. Beat at medium speed with a heavy-duty electric mixer for 5 minutes. (Or knead by hand on a lightly floured surface about 5 minutes.) Cover bowl, and let rise in a warm place (85°), free from drafts, 45 to 60 minutes or until doubled in bulk.

Punch dough down; divide in half, and place on a floured surface. Sprinkle each half with 1 tablespoon chopped fresh rosemary; knead rosemary into dough. Shape dough into 2 (8-inch) disks, and place each disk in a 9-inch cake pan coated with cooking spray. Brush each disk with 1 to 2 tablespoons olive oil. Sprinkle each with ½ tablespoon fresh rosemary. Let rise in a warm place (85°), free from drafts, 45 minutes.

Preheat oven to 400°. When dough has risen, bake at 400° for 20 minutes or until crust is lightly browned. Sprinkle additional olive oil over hot loaf, if desired. **Yield:** 2 loaves.

proofing the dough

Most yeast breads require proofing, a period of time in a warm place when the yeast produces carbon dioxide, which causes the dough to rise. The ideal place for proofing is a draft-free place with a temperature of 85°. You can create this kind of environment by placing the bowl of dough (covered with a barely damp kitchen towel or lightly greased plastic wrap) in an unheated oven with a pan of very hot water placed on the rack under the dough. Or place the bowl of dough along with a small bowl filled with very hot water in a microwave oven. Either way, be sure not to turn on the oven while the dough is rising.

Shrimp and grits may be the most recognized grits entrée in restaurants from coast to coast, but chefs and home cooks alike team grits with beef, pork, chicken, fish, and even gator. Both grits and cornmeal star in comfort foods such as Burgundy Beef

main dishes

Stew with Cornmeal-Thyme Dumplings and Grits Jambalaya as well as in edgy new dishes like Lime-Marinated Shrimp with Bean and Mango Salsa over Grilled Grits Cakes. And Cheesy Herbed Polenta takes its natural place, paired with Italian-seasoned dishes like Eggplant Parmesan.

Easy Pork Grillades over
Panko-Crusted Grits Patties

Famous for its highly seasoned Creole and Cajun recipes, Louisiana claims grillades and grits as one of its favorite traditional breakfast and brunch dishes. Here grillades (pronounced "gree odds") are served over Panko-Crusted Grits Patties, but for a more traditional dish, serve the pork over Asiago or Parmesan Grits (page 122). This version of grillades is pleasantly spicy—if you want a noticeable kick, go with the larger amount of crushed red pepper or add a splash of hot sauce. If you don't have fresh thyme or oregano, just use about a third as much dried.

Panko-Crusted Grits Patties
1¼ pounds boneless pork loin chops
¼ cup all-purpose flour
2 teaspoons Old Bay seasoning
4 tablespoons olive oil, divided
1 cup chopped celery
½ cup chopped green bell pepper
½ cup chopped red bell pepper

2 cups sliced baby bella mushrooms
1 (14.5-ounce) can diced tomatoes with garlic and onion, undrained
½ cup less-sodium chicken broth
1½ teaspoons fresh thyme leaves
1 teaspoon chopped fresh oregano
¼ to ½ teaspoon crushed red pepper
¼ teaspoon salt

Prepare Panko-Crusted Grits Patties. While patties are baking, slice pork crosswise into thin strips. Combine flour and seasoning; dredge pork in flour mixture. Heat 2 tablespoons oil in a large skillet over medium-high heat. Add half of pork; cook 3 minutes on each side or until browned. Remove from skillet; repeat procedure with 1 tablespoon oil and remaining pork.

Add remaining 1 tablespoon oil to skillet, and heat. Add celery and bell peppers; sauté 30 seconds. Add mushrooms; sauté 2 minutes. Add tomatoes and next 5 ingredients; cook over medium heat 5 minutes. Add pork; cover, reduce heat, and simmer 5 minutes. Serve over grits patties. **Yield:** 6 servings.

Panko-Crusted Grits Patties

This recipe yields 12 crusty grits patties—enough for a generous 2 patties per serving. But if you'd prefer only 1 patty per serving, just cut the recipe in half, and spoon the cooked grits into an 8-inch pan instead.

6 cups water
2 cups uncooked stone-ground grits
2 teaspoons salt
1 cup (4 ounces) freshly grated Parmesan cheese

2 large eggs, lightly beaten
¼ cup water
1½ cups panko (Japanese breadcrumbs)
½ teaspoon ground red pepper
Cooking spray

Combine 6 cups water, grits, and salt in a large, heavy saucepan; bring to a boil, stirring constantly. Reduce heat; simmer, uncovered, 20 to 25 minutes or until very thick, stirring often. Remove from heat; add Parmesan cheese, stirring until cheese melts. Spoon grits into a 13- x 9-inch baking pan lined with heavy-duty plastic wrap; cool 15 minutes. Place a dry paper towel over grits; cover pan, and chill 2 hours or until very firm.

Preheat oven to 425°. Turn chilled grits out onto a cutting board; remove plastic wrap, and cut grits into 12 squares. Combine eggs and ¼ cup water in a bowl, stirring with a fork to blend. Combine panko and red pepper in a second bowl. Dip grits patties into egg wash; dredge with panko mixture. Place panko-coated grits patties on a baking sheet coated with cooking spray. Bake at 425° for 25 minutes or until lightly browned. **Yield:** 12 patties.

Pork with Mushrooms and Two-Corn Grits

Fresh summer corn is best for Two-Corn Grits, but don't hesitate to try this combination in the winter months, too. I like to add a sprinkling of sugar to the grits to bring out the sweet corn flavor, especially if using frozen corn.

two-corn grits:

Melt 1 tablespoon butter in a medium, heavy saucepan; add 1¼ cups fresh corn kernels or thawed frozen corn, and sauté over medium-high heat 2 minutes. Remove corn from pan. Add 3 cups water and ¾ teaspoon salt to pan, and bring to a boil; gradually whisk in ¾ cup uncooked stone-ground grits. Reduce heat, and simmer, uncovered, 20 to 25 minutes or until thick, stirring often. Stir in corn, 1 tablespoon chopped fresh chives, ½ teaspoon sugar, and ¼ teaspoon pepper. Yield: 4 servings.

Two-Corn Grits (at left)

1 pound pork tenderloin, trimmed and cut into ½- to ¾-inch slices

¼ teaspoon salt

¼ teaspoon black pepper

3 tablespoons extra virgin olive oil, divided

1 (8-ounce) package fresh mushrooms, sliced

¾ cup less-sodium chicken broth

½ cup white wine

1½ teaspoons fresh thyme leaves or ½ teaspoon dried thyme

¼ teaspoon salt

¼ teaspoon black pepper

1 tablespoon plus 1 teaspoon cornstarch

2 tablespoons water

Prepare Two-Corn Grits; keep warm. While grits are cooking, sprinkle pork with ¼ teaspoon salt and ¼ teaspoon pepper. Heat 1 tablespoon oil in a large skillet over medium-high heat; add half of pork, and cook 2 to 3 minutes on each side or until browned. Remove from skillet; repeat procedure with 1 tablespoon oil and remaining pork.

Add remaining 1 tablespoon oil to skillet, and heat; add mushrooms, and cook over medium heat 5 minutes. Add broth and next 4 ingredients, stirring to loosen particles from bottom of skillet. Combine cornstarch and 2 tablespoons water, stirring until blended. Add cornstarch mixture to skillet, and bring to a boil. Cook 1 minute or until thick and bubbly, stirring constantly. Return pork to skillet; serve pork mixture over Two-Corn Grits. **Yield:** 4 servings.

Short Ribs Braised in Red Wine with Creamy Corn Grits

David Dickensauge, Executive Chef,

The Restaurant at Tria Market, Homewood, Alabama

4   pounds meaty beef short ribs
Salt to taste
Black pepper to taste
3   tablespoons butter, divided
2   tablespoons vegetable oil, divided
1   large onion, coarsely chopped
1   celery rib, coarsely chopped
1   large carrot, coarsely chopped
4   large garlic cloves, peeled and
    crushed
1   (750-milliliter) bottle red wine
    (such as pinot noir or merlot)
3   fresh thyme sprigs
4   fresh parsley sprigs
1   bay leaf
½   cup chopped fresh parsley, divided
Creamy Corn Grits with Butternut
    Squash and Sweet Corn

Season ribs with salt and pepper to taste (about ½ teaspoon each). Heat 1 tablespoon each of butter and oil in a heavy Dutch oven over high heat. Add ribs to pan in batches; cook each batch of ribs 10 minutes or until browned, turning as needed. Remove ribs, and set aside. Drain fat, and carefully wipe pan clean.

Preheat oven to 350°. Heat 1 tablespoon each of butter and oil in pan; add onion, celery, carrot, garlic, a large pinch of salt, and pepper to taste. Sauté 10 minutes. Add wine and next 3 ingredients; bring to a boil. Remove from heat, and add ribs to pan; cover tightly, and bake at 350° for 2 to 2½ hours, turning meat and recovering pan tightly every 30 to 45 minutes. (The meat should be very tender, falling off the bone.) Transfer ribs to a platter; strain liquid from pan into a saucepan, pressing hard on vegetables to extract all their juices. Discard vegetables and herbs.

Cover and chill strained liquid. After liquid has chilled, remove hardened fat. Bring cooking liquid to a boil; whisk in remaining 1 tablespoon butter, and cook until slightly thickened. Add ribs and ¼ cup chopped parsley; cook until ribs are thoroughly heated. Serve ribs over Creamy Corn Grits with Butternut Squash and Sweet Corn; sprinkle evenly with remaining ¼ cup parsley. **Yield:** 4 servings.

Creamy Corn Grits with Butternut Squash and Sweet Corn

1	cup peeled, diced butternut squash	2	tablespoons freshly grated Parmigiano-Reggiano cheese
1	cup fresh corn kernels	2	tablespoons minced fresh chives
2½	cups milk		Pinch of ground red pepper
2	tablespoons minced onion		Salt to taste
1	teaspoon minced garlic		Black pepper to taste
½	cup uncooked stone-ground yellow grits		
½	cup (2 ounces) shredded white Cheddar cheese		

Cook squash in boiling water to cover 5 minutes or just until tender. Remove with a slotted spoon, and set aside. Return water in pan to a boil; add corn. Cook 1 minute; drain and set aside.

Combine milk and next 2 ingredients in a medium, heavy saucepan; cook over medium-high heat just until mixture starts to boil. Gradually add grits, stirring with a wooden spoon; reduce heat, and simmer, uncovered, 20 to 25 minutes or until thick, stirring often. Remove from heat, and add cheeses, chives, and ground red pepper, stirring until cheeses melt. Season to taste with salt (about ½ teaspoon) and pepper (about ⅛ teaspoon). Sprinkle squash and corn over grits, and serve immediately. **Yield:** 4 servings.

flavorful, fresh herbs

Wouldn't you love to know the secrets of experienced chefs at the finest restaurants? One characteristic common to many of the chef's recipes submitted for this book is that they depend on fresh herbs to achieve just the right amount of seasoning in everything from main dishes to sauces, and, of course, grits. You can usually substitute a third as much dried herbs for fresh, but to a gourmet palate, the resulting flavor doesn't compare.

Grits Jambalaya

Believing that corn is the South's favorite grain, I like to substitute grits for the traditional rice in this quick and easy jambalaya. For a lighter version, use smoked turkey sausage instead of regular smoked sausage.

½ tablespoon olive oil
Cooking spray
1 pound smoked sausage, cut into ¼-inch slices
1 cup chopped onion
1 cup chopped green bell pepper
1 large garlic clove, minced

2 cups less-sodium beef broth
1 (14½-ounce) can diced tomatoes, undrained
¼ teaspoon dried thyme
⅛ teaspoon ground red pepper
1 cup uncooked stone-ground grits
1 cup chopped cooked chicken breast

Heat oil in a Dutch oven coated with cooking spray over medium-high heat. Add sausage, onion, bell pepper, and garlic to pan; sauté 5 minutes or until lightly browned. Add broth, tomatoes, thyme, and red pepper; bring to a boil. Add grits; cover, reduce heat to low, and cook 20 to 25 minutes or until thick, stirring often. Add chicken to pan, and cook 2 minutes or until thoroughly heated. **Yield:** 4 to 6 servings.

Southwestern Grits-Stuffed Peppers

Use whatever color bell peppers you have for this easy family dinner. My preference is to use both red and yellow.

2 cups water
½ teaspoon salt
½ cup uncooked stone-ground yellow or white grits
4 medium bell peppers
Cooking spray
½ pound lean ground beef
¼ cup chopped onion

¼ teaspoon salt
1 (10-ounce) can diced tomatoes and green chiles, drained
½ cup rinsed, drained canned black beans
½ cup (2 ounces) shredded reduced-fat Mexican four-cheese blend, divided

Bring water and ½ teaspoon salt to a boil in a small, heavy saucepan. Gradually whisk in grits; reduce heat, and simmer, uncovered, 20 to 25 minutes or until thick, stirring often.

While grits are cooking, preheat oven to 350°. Cut tops off bell peppers, and remove seeds. Drop peppers into a pan of boiling water, and cook 2 to 3 minutes. Remove from pan, and rinse with cold water; set aside.

Heat a skillet over medium-high heat. Coat skillet with cooking spray. Add beef and onion, and cook over medium-high heat 6 minutes or until beef is browned; drain, if needed. Season beef mixture with ¼ teaspoon salt. Add cooked grits, tomatoes, beans, and ¼ cup cheese to beef mixture; spoon into peppers, and place in a small baking dish. Bake at 350° for 20 minutes. Remove peppers from oven, and sprinkle with remaining ¼ cup cheese; bake 3 more minutes or until cheese melts. **Yield:** 4 servings.

Burgundy Beef Stew with Cornmeal-Thyme Dumplings

*A wide Dutch oven or deep sauté
pan works best here—allowing
enough room for the dumplings to
cook. I've also used these herb-
flavored dumplings (instead of the
more traditional biscuit dough) for
chicken and dumplings. I prefer using
fresh thyme, but during the winter,
when my herb garden is bare, I substitute about three-fourths as much dried
thyme for the fresh.*

1   tablespoon olive oil
1   pound round steak, trimmed and
    cut into 1-inch cubes
2   garlic cloves, minced
4   cups less-sodium beef broth
1   cup dry red wine (such as Burgundy)
2   tablespoons tomato paste
2¼ teaspoons fresh thyme leaves
¾   pound new potatoes, quartered

5   carrots, peeled and cut into 1-inch
    pieces
1   onion, cut into wedges
½   (8-ounce) package whole fresh
    mushrooms, cut into halves
½   teaspoon salt
½   teaspoon black pepper
    Cornmeal-Thyme Dumplings
    Additional fresh thyme leaves (optional)

Heat oil in a Dutch oven, sauté pan, or deep skillet over high heat. Add beef
and garlic, and sauté 5 to 7 minutes or until beef is browned. Add broth,
wine, tomato paste, and thyme; bring to a boil. Cover, reduce heat, and simmer 1½ hours or until steak is tender. Add potatoes and next 5 ingredients;
simmer, uncovered, 30 minutes or until vegetables are almost tender.

Scoop dough for dumplings by rounded tablespoons onto top of stew; cook
over low heat, uncovered, 10 minutes. Cover and cook 18 to 20 minutes or
until dumplings are done. (Avoid boiling mixture to prevent dumplings
from falling apart.) Garnish with thyme leaves, if desired. **Yield:** 4 servings.

Cornmeal-Thyme Dumplings

¾   cup stone-ground white or yellow
    cornmeal
¾   cup bread flour
1½ teaspoons baking powder

¾   teaspoon salt
2   to 3 teaspoons chopped fresh thyme
3   tablespoons butter, melted
½   cup milk

Combine cornmeal, bread flour, baking powder, salt, and thyme in a bowl
until well blended. Add butter and milk, stirring to blend. Cook as directed
in main recipe. **Yield:** 12 dumplings.

L.A. Gator and Smoked Bama Grits

Steve Zucker, Executive Chef, Baumhower's Wings Restaurant,

Mobile, Birmingham (Hoover), Tuscaloosa, Huntsville,

Montgomery, and Daphne, Alabama

chef's recipe

Chef Zucker shared this tip: "On the rare occasion you have any grits left over, they are even better sautéed! Pour them into an appropriately sized, lightly greased baking pan. Refrigerate until the next meal, then cut them into brownie-sized squares. Coat with a seasoned flour, dip in buttermilk, and then back in the flour. Sauté over medium heat in melted butter until brown; flip and brown the other side. I love this topped with sautéed shrimp in a spicy cream sauce."

smoked Bama grits:

Bring 6 cups water, 2 tablespoons butter, and 1½ teaspoons salt to a boil in a large, heavy saucepan; gradually whisk in 1¾ cups organic stone-ground yellow grits. Reduce heat; simmer, uncovered, 20 to 25 minutes or until thick, stirring often. Remove from heat; add 1¼ pounds shredded smoked Gouda cheese, stirring until cheese melts. Yield: 6 to 8 servings.

In Alabama, L.A. doesn't refer to the city in California—we all know it as "Lower Alabama," where chefs use Creole-type seasonings. I first tasted this delicious dish served over a bowl of Smoked Bama Grits at the "Kiss My Grits!" benefit dinner in Montgomery, Alabama (see page 31), and was thrilled to get a copy of the recipe.

½ cup canola oil
½ cup all-purpose flour
1½ pounds alligator tail meat, cut into 1-inch pieces (or substitute chicken)
8 ounces chopped smoked sausage (such as Conecuh)
1½ cups chopped onion
1 cup chopped celery
½ cup chopped bell pepper
2 tablespoons minced garlic
2 tablespoons minced jalapeño pepper

4 cups water
1 cup chopped tomatoes
½ cup dry white wine
1 tablespoon Worcestershire sauce
1 tablespoon hot sauce (such as Crystal)
¼ cup chopped fresh parsley
¼ cup sliced green onions
1½ teaspoons black pepper
1 tablespoon Creole seasoning (such as Tony Chachere's)
Smoked Bama Grits (at left)

Heat oil in a large cast-iron pot over medium heat; whisk in flour, and cook, whisking constantly, to make a dark brown roux (10 to 15 minutes). Add alligator or chicken to roux; cook over medium-high heat 2 minutes or until meat starts to brown, stirring constantly. Add smoked sausage, and cook 2 minutes. Add onion, celery, and bell pepper; cook 3 minutes, stirring often. Add garlic and jalapeño pepper, and cook 2 minutes, stirring constantly; gradually stir in 4 cups water. Add tomatoes, wine, Worcestershire sauce, and hot sauce. Bring mixture to a boil; reduce heat, and simmer 1½ to 2 hours, stirring occasionally. Add parsley, green onions, black pepper, and Creole seasoning. Serve over Smoked Bama Grits. **Yield:** 6 to 8 servings.

Mexican Cornmeal-Crusted Chicken Pie

1 (16-ounce) jar salsa
1 (15-ounce) can black beans, rinsed and drained
1 (14.5-ounce) can diced tomatoes, undrained
2 cups frozen whole kernel corn
2 teaspoons chili powder
2 cups chopped cooked chicken breast
2 tablespoons chopped fresh cilantro
2 tablespoons fresh lime juice
Cooking spray
1 tablespoon butter
½ cup chopped onion
1 cup stone-ground cornmeal
¼ cup all-purpose flour
1½ teaspoons baking powder
½ teaspoon salt
1 cup (4 ounces) shredded Monterey Jack cheese
1 egg, lightly beaten
1 (4.5-ounce) can chopped green chiles, drained
1½ cups buttermilk

This Southwestern-flavored chicken pot pie adds cheese and chiles to a basic cornbread batter. If you're cooking the chicken yourself, start with about 1 pound uncooked boneless chicken breast to get 2 cups chopped cooked chicken. Or if you're in a hurry, you can start with rotisserie chicken from your grocery's deli.

Preheat oven to 375°. Combine first 5 ingredients in a large saucepan over medium heat; cook 10 minutes, stirring occasionally. Stir in chicken, cilantro, and lime juice; spoon into a 13- x 9-inch baking dish coated with cooking spray.

While salsa mixture is cooking, melt butter in a small skillet; add onion, and sauté 3 minutes. Combine cornmeal, flour, baking powder, and salt in a large bowl until well blended; stir in cheese. Combine onion, egg, green chiles, and buttermilk; add to cornmeal mixture, stirring well. Spoon cornmeal mixture over hot chicken mixture. Bake at 375° for 40 to 45 minutes or until crust is lightly browned. Let stand 10 minutes before serving.
Yield: 6 to 8 servings.

Southwestern Pizza with Cornmeal Crust

1 (¼-ounce) envelope rapid-rise yeast (2¼ teaspoons)
1⅔ cups warm water (100° to 110°)
1 tablespoon sugar
3 tablespoons olive oil, divided
1¼ teaspoons salt
2¾ to 3 cups bread flour
1⅓ cups stone-ground cornmeal
¾ pound chicken tenderloins
Cooking spray
2 tablespoons fresh lime juice
¼ teaspoon salt
1½ cups black bean and corn salsa
1 cup chopped red bell pepper
½ cup sliced black olives
2 cups (8 ounces) shredded Monterey Jack cheese
1 cup (4 ounces) shredded sharp Cheddar cheese
¼ cup chopped fresh cilantro

It's a tradition in my home to make homemade pizza on Saturday nights— usually with a whole wheat crust, Italian pizza sauce, and toppings. But after trying this cornmeal-crusted pizza with Southwestern toppings, we have a rival to our traditional favorite.

Combine yeast and water, stirring to dissolve; let stand 2 to 3 minutes. Whisk together yeast mixture, sugar, 2 tablespoons olive oil, and 1¼ teaspoons salt in a large mixing bowl. Add 2¾ cups flour and cornmeal, adding additional flour as needed to make a soft dough; beat at medium speed with a heavy-duty electric mixer until ingredients are well mixed and dough is stiff. Cover dough; let rise in a warm place (85°), free from drafts, 45 minutes or until doubled in bulk.

While dough is rising, preheat oven to 350°. Place chicken in an 11- x 7-inch baking dish coated with cooking spray; sprinkle with lime juice, remaining 1 tablespoon olive oil, and ¼ teaspoon salt. Bake at 350° for 20 minutes or until chicken is done. Let chicken cool, and shred into bite-size pieces.

Increase oven temperature to 425°. Divide dough in half, and place on a heavily floured surface. Shape each dough half into a round disk, and roll to a 12-inch diameter with a floured rolling pin. Place each round of dough on a 12-inch pizza pan coated with cooking spray. Spread about ¾ cup salsa over each crust; top each crust with half each of shredded chicken, bell pepper, and black olives. Bake at 425° for 10 to 12 minutes; sprinkle each pizza with half of each type of cheese, and bake 8 to 10 more minutes or until crust is lightly browned. Sprinkle pizzas with cilantro. **Yield:** 2 (12-inch) pizzas.

1 large pizza:
To make 1 large pizza, roll all of dough into a 15- x 10-inch rectangle, and place on a 15- x 10-inch jelly-roll pan coated with cooking spray. Assemble pizza as directed at left, and bake at 425° for 13 minutes. Add cheese, and bake 10 to 12 more minutes.

Turkey-Corn Chili with Cheddar Cornmeal Waffles

For a hearty meal on a chilly day, you'll actually get a triple dose of corn in this recipe combo: stone-ground grits (from dried corn) and fresh-cut corn in the chili, along with the stone-ground cornmeal in the cheesy waffles.

1   tablespoon olive oil
1¼ pounds ground turkey breast
1   bell pepper, chopped
½   cup chopped onion
1   (14-ounce) can less-sodium chicken broth
1   (14½-ounce) can no-salt-added diced tomatoes, undrained
1   (10-ounce) can diced tomatoes and green chiles, undrained
½   cup uncooked stone-ground yellow or white grits

1½ to 2 tablespoons chili powder
1   teaspoon salt
¼   to ½ teaspoon black pepper
2   bay leaves
1   (15-ounce) can black beans, rinsed and drained
1½ cups fresh corn kernels (about 3 ears) or frozen whole kernel corn, thawed
Cheddar Cornmeal Waffles

Heat oil in a Dutch oven over medium-high heat. Add turkey, bell pepper, and onion; cook 8 to 10 minutes or until turkey is done, stirring to crumble. Add broth and next 7 ingredients; bring to a boil, stirring often. Cover, reduce heat, and simmer 20 minutes, stirring occasionally. Add beans and corn; cook 15 minutes, stirring occasionally. Remove and discard bay leaves. Serve chili with or atop Cheddar Cornmeal Waffles. **Yield:** 5 to 6 servings.

Cheddar Cornmeal Waffles

2   cups buttermilk
1   large egg, lightly beaten
¼   cup vegetable oil
3   cups stone-ground yellow or white cornmeal
2   teaspoons sugar

1   teaspoon baking powder
½   teaspoon baking soda
1   teaspoon salt
1   cup (4 ounces) finely shredded Cheddar cheese
Cooking spray

easy cornbread crisps:
For another tasty accompaniment to the Turkey-Corn Chili, bake a batch of Easy Cornbread Crisps (page 68).

Combine buttermilk, egg, and oil in a medium bowl. Combine cornmeal and next 4 ingredients in a separate large bowl; stir in cheese. Add buttermilk mixture to cornmeal mixture, stirring gently, just until dry ingredients are moistened. Pour about 1¼ cups batter onto a preheated 8-inch square waffle iron lightly coated with cooking spray. Cook waffles 2 minutes or until lightly browned. **Yield:** 10 to 12 (4-inch square) waffles.

Note: As waffles become done, remove them from the waffle iron to a wire rack so that waffles do not become soggy from the steam that forms when hot waffles are placed immediately on a plate.

Easy Italian Sausage over Garlic Polenta

12 ounces Italian turkey sausage

Cooking spray

1 cup chopped red bell pepper

3 garlic cloves, minced and divided

1 (8-ounce) package fresh mushrooms, sliced

1 (14½-ounce) can no-salt-added diced tomatoes, undrained

1 (8-ounce) can tomato sauce with basil, garlic, and oregano

2 teaspoons sugar

1 teaspoon olive oil

3 cups water

½ teaspoon salt

¾ cup uncooked stone-ground white or yellow polenta

½ cup (2 ounces) shredded Parmesan cheese

Additional shredded Parmesan cheese (optional)

Chopped fresh basil (optional)

Here's a family favorite because it's quick, healthy, and satisfying. All that's needed to round out the meal is a green salad and crusty bread. A good supply of canned tomatoes in the pantry comes in handy for quick recipes like this. A secret to preparing sauces with canned tomatoes is to add a touch of sugar to counteract any metallic taste.

Remove and discard casing from sausage. Heat a large skillet over medium-high heat, and coat pan with cooking spray. Add sausage, bell pepper, and 1 garlic clove; cook 5 minutes, stirring to crumble sausage. Add mushrooms, and sauté 5 minutes or until turkey is browned and mushrooms are tender. Add tomatoes, tomato sauce, and sugar; bring to a boil. Reduce heat, and simmer 15 minutes, stirring occasionally.

While sausage mixture is cooking, heat oil in a medium, heavy saucepan over medium heat. Add remaining 2 minced garlic cloves; sauté 1 minute. Add water and salt; bring to a boil. Gradually whisk in polenta. Reduce heat, and simmer, uncovered, 12 to 14 minutes, stirring occasionally. Remove from heat, and add ½ cup shredded Parmesan cheese, stirring until cheese melts. Serve sausage mixture over polenta; garnish with additional shredded Parmesan cheese and basil, if desired. **Yield:** 3 to 4 servings.

Grilled Quail with Corn Polenta Cakes

Gary Donlick, Executive Chef, Pano's and Paul's, Atlanta, Georgia

chef's recipe

According to Chef Donlick, "Be careful not to overcook the quail. Boneless quail cooks very fast and will continue to cook off the grill, so cook the breast to a medium degree of doneness." While I would prepare this upscale Southern recipe as an entrée, Gary serves one quail atop two polenta cakes as an appetizer. He accompanies the quail and polenta cakes with a small salad of arugula, dressed with freshly squeezed lemon, olive oil, and shaved fresh Parmesan cheese.

the South's favorite game bird

If there's a hunter in your family, you might have a ready supply of quail. But if not, check with a specialty foods market or butcher shop. Remember to follow Chef Donlick's advice and avoid overcooking the lean, delicately flavored meat.

2 cups water	6 cups chicken stock
Kosher salt to taste	1 cup heavy whipping cream
1 teaspoon sugar	2 cups uncooked stone-ground polenta
1 cup fresh corn kernels	1 cup freshly grated Parmesan cheese
2 ounces pancetta or bacon, diced	6 quail, boned
2 tablespoons minced shallots	2 tablespoons olive oil
2 tablespoons chopped fresh sage	1 tablespoon chopped fresh thyme
4 tablespoons unsalted butter, divided	Black pepper to taste

Line a 13- x 9-inch baking pan with parchment paper or heavy-duty plastic wrap; set aside. Bring water, kosher salt to taste (about 1 teaspoon), and sugar to a boil in a small saucepan. Add corn, and cook 5 minutes; drain.

Sauté pancetta in a large, heavy saucepot over medium heat 5 minutes or until browned and almost crispy. Add shallots, and cook 2 minutes. Add sage and 2 tablespoons butter, stirring until butter melts. Add chicken stock and cream to pan. Bring to a boil, and slowly whisk in polenta. Reduce heat, and simmer 12 minutes or until very thick, whisking often. Remove from heat; add corn and Parmesan cheese. Season to taste with kosher salt (about ½ teaspoon). Pour polenta into prepared pan; cover and chill until very firm.

Turn chilled polenta out onto a cutting board; remove paper, and cut the polenta with a 2½- to 3-inch round biscuit cutter into 12 circles. Heat a large, nonstick sauté pan or skillet over medium heat. Add butter (1 tablespoon per batch), and cook the cakes in batches 5 to 6 minutes or until golden brown on each side; keep warm.

Preheat grill to 350° to 400° (medium-high). Brush quail with olive oil and sprinkle with thyme; season to taste with salt and pepper. Grill, covered with grill lid, over medium-high heat (350° to 400°) about 2 minutes on each side. Serve over polenta cakes. **Yield:** 3 main-dish or 6 appetizer servings.

Eggplant Parmesan with Cheesy Herbed Polenta

Here's a tasty meatless main dish that'll help stretch the food budget. Instead of serving Eggplant Parmesan the traditional way over pasta, try it over this cheesy, herb-flavored polenta.

2   large eggs
1   tablespoon water
½   cup stone-ground cornmeal
½   cup fine, dry breadcrumbs
1   teaspoon dried Italian herbs
1   eggplant (about 1 pound), cut into ½-inch slices
¼   teaspoon salt
⅛   teaspoon black pepper

6   tablespoons olive oil, divided
Cooking spray
½   cup (2 ounces) shredded mozzarella cheese, divided
¾   cup (3 ounces) freshly grated Parmesan cheese, divided
1½ cups commercial pasta sauce
Cheesy Herbed Polenta (at right)

Preheat oven to 375°. Lightly whisk eggs and water in a shallow dish. In another shallow dish, combine cornmeal and next 2 ingredients. Sprinkle both sides of eggplant with salt and pepper. Dip eggplant slices in egg mixture, and dredge in cornmeal mixture.

Heat 3 tablespoons olive oil in a large skillet over medium heat. Place half of eggplant slices in a single layer in skillet; cook 2 minutes on each side or until lightly browned and tender. Repeat procedure with remaining olive oil and eggplant.

Arrange half of eggplant in an 11- x 7-inch baking dish coated with cooking spray; sprinkle with ¼ cup mozzarella cheese and ¼ cup Parmesan cheese. Repeat layers, and top with pasta sauce. Cover and bake at 375° for 30 minutes. Uncover and sprinkle with remaining ¼ cup Parmesan cheese. Serve immediately over Cheesy Herbed Polenta. **Yield:** 4 servings.

cheesy herbed polenta:

Combine 2 cups water, 2 cups milk, and 1 teaspoon salt in a large, heavy saucepan; cook over medium-high heat just until mixture starts to boil. Gradually whisk in 1 cup uncooked stone-ground polenta. Reduce heat, and simmer, uncovered, 12 to 14 minutes or until thick, stirring often. Remove from heat, and add 1½ teaspoons dried Italian herbs and 1 cup (4 ounces) shredded mozzarella cheese, stirring until cheese melts. Cover polenta, and keep warm. Yield: 4 servings.

Chutney Salmon with Almond-Raisin Grits

A curried mango chutney sauce is a delicious complement to the almond- and raisin-studded grits.

The speckled grits produced by some grtismills are so called because they are a mixture of yellow and white grits.

Almond-Raisin Grits
1   cup white wine (such as Reisling)
1   (9-ounce) jar prepared mango chutney
¼   cup cider vinegar
2   teaspoons curry powder
¼   teaspoon salt

4   (6-ounce) salmon fillets (about 1-inch thick)
Cooking spray
¼   teaspoon salt
¼   to ½ teaspoon freshly ground black pepper
2 green onions, chopped

Prepare Almond-Raisin Grits; set aside, and keep warm. While grits are cooking, combine wine and next 4 ingredients in a medium skillet; bring to a boil over medium heat, stirring often. Reduce heat; simmer 5 to 6 minutes or until sauce is reduced by about half. Set aside, and keep warm.

Preheat broiler. Place salmon, skin side down, on a broiler pan coated with cooking spray. Sprinkle salmon with ¼ teaspoon salt and pepper. Broil 5 minutes; brush with a thin layer of chutney sauce. Broil 4 to 5 more minutes or until fish flakes with a fork. Serve salmon and remaining chutney sauce over Almond-Raisin Grits. Sprinkle with green onions. **Yield:** 4 servings.

Almond-Raisin Grits

4   cups water
1   teaspoon salt
1   cup uncooked stone-ground speckled, white, or yellow grits

½   cup golden raisins
1   tablespoon butter
¼   cup slivered almonds, toasted
¼   to ½ teaspoon black pepper

Bring water and salt to a boil in a medium, heavy saucepan; gradually whisk in grits. Reduce heat; simmer 18 minutes. Stir in raisins, and continue to cook 5 to 7 minutes or until thick, stirring often. Remove from heat; add butter, stirring to melt. Stir in almonds and pepper. **Yield:** 4 servings.

Fried Catfish

Like many Southerners, I have enjoyed more than one catfish dinner. In fact, I remember my grandfather Lester talking about a huge catfish that he caught in his lake, cleaned, and asked Mama to fry. Through the years, the weight of the catfish grew and grew, along with the amount of cornmeal and oil reportedly needed for dredging and frying the fish. Now that I'm older and wiser, I wonder how big the catfish really was. And I wonder about the tenderness of a catfish that size! But I will admit—Papa did tell a captivating story, and isn't that the goal of most fishermen?

Vegetable oil
About 1 cup buttermilk
4   (6-ounce) catfish fillets
¾   cup stone-ground cornmeal
¼   cup all-purpose flour

1   teaspoon salt
¾   teaspoon garlic powder
¾   teaspoon ground red pepper
¼   teaspoon black pepper
Old-Fashioned Hush Puppies (page 68)

Pour oil to a depth of 1½ inches into a large, deep skillet; place over high heat. While oil is heating, place buttermilk in a shallow bowl or pie plate. Place catfish in bowl, turning to coat well; let catfish stand in buttermilk while oil heats.

Combine cornmeal and next 5 ingredients in a shallow dish or zip-top plastic bag. Remove catfish from buttermilk, allowing excess buttermilk to drip off fish; dredge fish in cornmeal mixture. Fry fillets in hot oil (about 350° to 375°) for 3 to 4 minutes or until golden. Drain on wire racks over paper towels. Serve with Old-Fashioned Hush Puppies. **Yield:** 4 servings.

Cornmeal-Crusted Grouper with Southern Tomato Gravy

Angela Schmidt, Executive Chef, John's City Diner, Birmingham, Alabama

chef's recipe

Chef Schmidt remembers her own fried fish stories from childhood. She wrote, "This recipe is inspired by my grandmother, Grace Luby of Columbus, Georgia, who made a very similar dish when I was young. The brightness of the gravy complements the crispy cornmeal crust." And like most expert cooks, Angela knows one of the most important points to remember in cooking fish is to avoid overcooking. That's why she recommends using an instant-read thermometer to determine the doneness of the fish—it's especially helpful when cooking a thick piece of fish like grouper.

1 tablespoon olive oil	1½ teaspoons cracked black pepper
½ cup minced shallots	1 large egg, lightly beaten
4 fresh thyme sprigs	2 tablespoons water
2 (28-ounce) cans Italian plum tomatoes (about 1½ quarts), chopped	1¾ cups stone-ground cornmeal
1 lemon, thinly sliced	2 tablespoons table salt
3 tablespoons cornstarch	2 teaspoons black pepper
¼ cup half-and-half	½ teaspoon cayenne pepper
2 teaspoons kosher salt	4 (8-ounce) fillets black grouper
	All-purpose flour (about ½ cup)
	¼ cup olive oil

For the gravy, heat a sauté pan or large skillet over medium-high heat; add 1 tablespoon olive oil. Add shallots and thyme; cook 3 minutes. Add tomatoes and lemon; bring to a boil. Reduce heat to medium; simmer 20 minutes.

In a small bowl, whisk together cornstarch and half-and-half to create a slurry. Remove lemon and thyme sprigs from sauté pan, and discard; whisk slurry into pan. Cook 1 to 2 minutes or until sauce thickens, whisking constantly. Season with 2 teaspoons kosher salt and 1½ teaspoons cracked pepper; keep warm.

For the fish, combine egg and water in a shallow dish, stirring to blend. In a separate shallow dish, combine cornmeal and next 3 ingredients. Pat fish dry with paper towels; dredge fish in flour, then dip in egg wash, and finally dredge in cornmeal mixture. (Discard remaining cornmeal mixture.) Heat ¼ cup olive oil in a large skillet over medium-high heat; add fish, and panfry 3 to 4 minutes on each side or until fish reaches an internal temperature of 125°. (Unless you have a really large skillet, you may need to cook the fish in batches. If so, add more olive oil as needed.) Serve fish immediately with tomato gravy. **Yield:** 4 servings.

Bay Scallops and Mushrooms with Grits

Chefs Brian Williams and David Wurth, Local 111, Philmont, New York

4 cups water	3 cups whole oyster mushrooms, cleaned (about 8 ounces white button mushrooms, sliced in half lengthwise, may be substituted)
1 tablespoon butter	
1 cup uncooked stone-ground grits	
Kosher salt to taste	
6 to 8 tablespoons olive oil, divided	¼ cup butter, divided
1 tablespoon fresh thyme leaves, divided	1 pound bay scallops (not processed) or dry diver sea scallops
1 large shallot, finely chopped	½ cup white wine

For the grits, bring water and butter to a boil in a medium, heavy saucepan; whisk in grits. Reduce heat; simmer 25 minutes or until thick, stirring often. Remove from heat; season to taste with kosher salt (about 1½ teaspoons).

To prepare scallops and mushrooms, heat 2 tablespoons oil in a large cast-iron skillet over medium-high heat until oil is very hot. Add 1 teaspoon thyme and shallot; cook 1 minute, stirring constantly. Add mushrooms and 2 tablespoons butter. Cook, stirring constantly, 5 to 7 minutes or until mushrooms are soft and lightly browned. Pour mushrooms and liquid into a bowl, and set aside.

Wipe pan clean, and return to stovetop; add 2 tablespoons olive oil, and heat over medium-high heat until oil is very hot. Add scallops (in batches as they should be cooked uncrowded in a single layer). Turn scallops after 2 minutes, allowing them to brown well on both sides. After all scallops are cooked, add to mushrooms. Remove pan from heat, and let pan cool 1 minute; add wine. (It should sizzle and steam slightly.) Return pan to heat, and add remaining 2 tablespoons butter, allowing mixture to simmer until butter melts, scraping bottom of pan with a wooden spoon. Add mushrooms and scallops. Season to taste with kosher salt (about ¼ teaspoon). Spoon grits into 4 shallow bowls or dinner plates; spoon scallops, mushrooms, and sauce over grits. Garnish with remaining 2 teaspoons thyme. **Yield:** 4 servings.

chef's recipe

After sharing his recipe, Chef Williams explained his thoughts about grits outside of the South: "Polenta has been a long-time favorite of New Yorkers and somehow grits never became popular. I believe it is because we never had access to a high-quality product. Thanks to purveyors of stone-ground grits, we can now enjoy what Southerners have loved for generations." And Chef Wurth says, "Southern transplants who taste our grits when served with various accompaniments feel reconnected to some glorious lost flavors."

Busters and Grits

John Besh, Chef & Owner, Besh Restaurant Group
(August, Besh Steak, Lüke, La Provençe), New Orleans, Louisiana

chef's recipe

Chef Besh says that if you can't find small buster crabs, you can cut larger soft-shell crabs into fourths, and fry them as directed in his recipe. "Frying the crab quarters will yield every bit as much of a great dish."

what are buster crabs?

They're the crabs caught halfway through the process of shedding their hard shell, so they appear to be literally "busting" out of their shells. These live crabs are kept in tanks until their hard shells completely fall off and they become soft-shell crabs.

4	cups water
1	cup uncooked stone-ground white grits
6	tablespoons butter, divided
¼	cup mascarpone cheese
	Salt to taste
	Black pepper to taste
4	large eggs, lightly beaten
½	cup milk
1	cup stone-ground cornmeal
½	cup all-purpose flour
1	teaspoon Creole seasoning
6	small soft-shell blue crabs, cleaned and trimmed
4	cups canola oil
1	cup Crab Pan Sauce
3	garlic cloves, minced
1	green onion, chopped
2	dashes of Tabasco sauce

In a medium, heavy saucepan, bring 4 cups water to a boil; add grits, stirring constantly. Once the grits return to a boil, reduce heat to a low simmer; cover and cook 20 minutes, stirring occasionally. Remove from heat, and stir in 3 tablespoons butter and ¼ cup mascarpone cheese. Season to taste with salt (about 1 teaspoon) and black pepper; cover and keep warm.

In a mixing bowl, whisk together eggs, milk, cornmeal, flour, and Creole seasoning until smooth. Dip crabs into the cornmeal batter, and fry them, 1 at a time, in hot canola oil (350°) until golden brown; remove to absorbent paper towels, and season with an additional touch of salt.

Combine Crab Pan Sauce, garlic, and green onion in a medium saucepan. Bring to a boil; remove from heat, and stir in 3 tablespoons butter, Tabasco sauce, and salt and pepper to taste. To plate this dish, spoon grits into a bowl with a generous amount of the crab and green onion sauce ladled around the grits; place the fried soft shells over the grits, and serve immediately. **Yield:** 6 servings.

Crab Pan Sauce

1 tablespoon extra virgin olive oil
1 small onion, diced
2 garlic cloves, minced
¼ cup minced fennel
1 teaspoon crushed red pepper flakes
1 cup crab stock

Leaves from 1 fresh thyme sprig
1 fresh tarragon sprig
1 bay leaf
½ cup heavy whipping cream
½ cup dry vermouth

Heat oil in a medium, heavy saucepan over moderate heat; add onion, garlic, fennel, and red pepper flakes to the pan. Cook vegetable mixture 3 minutes, stirring often. Add crab stock and remaining ingredients to pan. Increase heat to high, and cook 10 to 12 minutes or until sauce is reduced by half. Remove and discard tarragon sprig and bay leaf. **Yield:** 1 cup.

crab stock:

Chef Besh prepares his own crab stock to have on hand for Crab Pan Sauce. You can make your own stock by cooking crab or shrimp shells in boiling water along with vegetables such as celery, onion, and garlic. After about an hour, remove the crab shells and strain the stock, discarding the shells and vegetables. Use the stock immediately, or cover and chill it to use within 2 days. You can also freeze the stock for up to a month.

For an easy substitute (or if you don't have crab shells), I recommend combining one shrimp or fish bouillon cube with 1 cup boiling water for 1 cup crab stock.

1. Give the crabs a generous coating of the seasoned cornmeal mixture before dropping them into hot oil.

2. Fry the crabs, 1 at a time, in hot oil until golden brown; use tongs to carefully remove each crab to paper towels to drain.

People who grew up in the low country of South Carolina are quite familiar with the most basic shrimp and grits recipe—shrimp sautéed in butter, then seasoned with bacon or ham, and served in a simple sauce over cooked stone-ground grits. The original creators of shrimp and grits made breakfast with what was readily available: shrimp caught by local fisherman and grits

shrimp & grits

ground at local gristmills. Over the years, shrimp and grits have become more sophisticated by the addition of ingredients like sautéed bell peppers, gourmet mushrooms, fancy sausages, wine, and herbs. No longer just for breakfast, these versions are perhaps more suited to evening meals and are increasingly served at the finest restaurants in the South and beyond.

Breakfast Shrimp and Grits

Southern favorite

This special section of shrimp and grits recipes starts with a breakfast-suitable recipe: simple enough for morning taste buds and easy enough for a morning schedule. (I personally prefer shrimp and grits at night, and this is one of my favorite recipes for a quick weeknight supper.)

4 cups water

1 teaspoon salt

1 cup uncooked stone-ground grits

1 to 2 tablespoons butter or heavy whipping cream

5 applewood-smoked bacon slices

1¼ pounds unpeeled medium-size or large raw shrimp, peeled and deveined

2 tablespoons all-purpose flour

1 cup less-sodium chicken broth

1 tablespoon fresh lemon juice

¼ teaspoon hot sauce

⅛ teaspoon salt

⅛ teaspoon black pepper

2 tablespoons heavy whipping cream

Bring water and 1 teaspoon salt to a boil in a medium, heavy saucepan; gradually whisk in grits. Reduce heat; simmer, uncovered, 20 to 25 minutes or until thick, stirring often. Remove from heat; stir in butter, and keep warm.

While grits are cooking, cook bacon in a large skillet over medium heat until crisp and browned. Remove and drain on paper towels, reserving 1 tablespoon drippings in skillet. Crumble bacon, and set aside.

Add shrimp to skillet; sauté over medium-high heat 3 minutes or until shrimp turn pink. Whisk together flour and broth until smooth. Add flour mixture, lemon juice, hot sauce, ⅛ teaspoon salt, and pepper to skillet; cook until mixture is thick and bubbly, stirring to loosen particles from bottom of skillet. Stir in cream and bacon, and cook just until thoroughly heated. Serve shrimp and sauce over hot grits. **Yield:** 4 servings.

Shrimp and Grits with Succotash

John Norman, Executive Chef,

Cuvee Beach Bistro & Wine Bar, Destin, Florida

4 cups water	½ cup water
1 teaspoon salt	¾ cup fresh corn kernels
1 cup uncooked stone-ground yellow grits	24 large raw shrimp, peeled and deveined
½ cup unsalted butter, divided	½ cup diced tasso ham
¼ cup (1 ounce) freshly grated Parmesan cheese	¼ cup diced shallot
2 tablespoons olive oil, divided	2 tablespoons white wine
¾ cup fresh lima beans	¾ cup grape tomato halves
¼ cup chopped onion	1 tablespoon fresh lemon juice
2 tablespoons chopped celery	⅛ teaspoon Tabasco sauce
2 tablespoons chopped carrot	Salt to taste
	Ground white pepper to taste

Bring 4 cups water and 1 teaspoon salt to a boil in a medium, heavy saucepan; gradually whisk in grits. Reduce heat; simmer, uncovered, 20 to 25 minutes or until thick, stirring often. Remove from heat, and add ¼ cup butter and Parmesan cheese, stirring until cheese melts; cover and keep warm.

Heat 1 tablespoon oil in a sauté pan or large skillet over medium-high heat; add lima beans, onion, celery, and carrot; sauté 2 minutes. Add ½ cup water; cover, reduce heat, and simmer 15 minutes. Add corn; cook, uncovered, 3 to 5 minutes. Remove vegetables from pan; keep warm.

Add remaining 1 tablespoon oil to pan, and heat; add shrimp, and cook 1 to 2 minutes on each side. Add ham and shallot; cook 2 minutes. Add white wine, and cook to deglaze pan (stirring to loosen particles from bottom of skillet). Add lima bean mixture and tomato halves to pan. Cook 1 to 2 minutes or until heated through. Stir in remaining ¼ cup butter, lemon juice, and Tabasco sauce; season to taste with salt (about ¼ teaspoon) and white pepper. Serve shrimp and succotash over hot grits. **Yield:** 4 servings.

chef's recipe

Chef Norman's Shrimp and Grits with Succotash is as pleasing to the palate as it is appealing to the eye—no surprise that it's a real hit on the Florida panhandle. I agree with John, who says that Shrimp and Grits with Succotash "is well suited for home cooks and the ingredients are fairly flexible. The tasso ham can be substituted with any spicy sausage such as andouille. Any type of tomatoes and any type of beans can be used." John insists on using stone-ground grits because they have "the flavor and aroma of fresh corn."

Garlic Shrimp with Edamame and Tomatoes over Asiago Grits

pictured on page 80

While Chef Norman's recipe for Shrimp and Grits with Succotash (page 113) is perfect for special occasions when preparation time and calories aren't a concern, I came up with a quicker, lighter version of his recipe for a hurry-up, more calorie-conscious meal. This version gets lots of flavor from garlic and lemon juice, and it features healthy edamame.

tasty, trendy edamame

Rich in fiber, low in fat, and full of healthy soy protein, edamame (green soybeans) add nutrition as well as color to main dishes and side dishes alike. Edamame look a lot like baby lima beans but have a sweeter, nuttier taste. You can find cooked, ready-to-eat edamame in refrigerated packages in the produce section of your grocery store. I love the texture edamame adds to this shrimp and grits dish, and also recommend tossing the bright green soybeans into fresh salads or grabbing a handful for a quick snack.

Asiago Grits (page 122)
¼   cup butter
4   large garlic cloves, minced
1⅓ pounds unpeeled large raw shrimp, peeled and deveined
½   cup refrigerated cooked edamame
½   cup grape tomato halves

¼   cup dry white wine
2   tablespoons fresh lemon juice
¼   teaspoon freshly ground black pepper
2   tablespoons minced fresh flat-leaf parsley

Prepare Asiago Grits; set aside, and keep warm.

While grits are cooking, melt butter in a large skillet; add garlic, and sauté 1 to 2 minutes. Add shrimp, and cook 3 minutes or until shrimp are almost done, stirring constantly. Remove shrimp from skillet.

Add edamame and next 4 ingredients to skillet; cook over high heat until sauce is reduced by about half. Return shrimp to skillet; cook until shrimp turn pink and mixture is thoroughly heated; stir in parsley. Serve shrimp mixture immediately over Asiago Grits. **Yield:** 4 servings.

Shrimp Creole over Green Onion Grits

Sauté green onions and garlic in olive oil before cooking the grits to accompany my easy version of Shrimp Creole or as a substitute for the Two-Corn Grits in the Pork with Mushrooms recipe on page 84. The simple flavors make Green Onion Grits an excellent side dish for many entrées.

Green Onion Grits (page 123)
Olive oil-flavored cooking spray
1   cup chopped celery (about 2 stalks)
½   cup chopped onion
1   garlic clove, minced
1   (14½-ounce) can diced tomatoes with zesty green chiles, undrained
1   (8-ounce) can no-salt-added tomato sauce
1½ teaspoons Creole seasoning (such as Emeril's Bayou Blast)
1¼ pounds unpeeled medium-size or large raw shrimp, peeled and deveined

Prepare Green Onion Grits; cover and keep warm.

While grits are cooking, heat a large skillet over medium-high heat; coat skillet with cooking spray. Add celery, onion, and garlic to skillet; coat vegetables with cooking spray, and sauté 3 to 4 minutes. Add tomatoes, tomato sauce, and Creole seasoning; bring to a boil. Reduce heat, and simmer 8 minutes.

Add shrimp to tomato mixture; cover and cook 3 minutes or until shrimp turn pink, stirring often. Serve shrimp mixture over grits.
Yield: 4 servings.

Creole and Cajun cuisine

Louisiana's legendary ancestors have created some of the South's favorite dishes, including shrimp Creole, grillades and grits, jambalaya, seafood gumbo, and crawfish étouffée. Creole dishes often rely on butter, cream, and tomatoes, while the more rustic Cajun dishes depend on pork fat and potent spices. Recipes from both cuisines, however, require green bell peppers, onions, and celery for seasoning.

Anniversary Shrimp and Grits

Southern favorite

When we celebrated Mother and Daddy's 60th wedding anniversary, we needed an outstanding entrée to match their outstanding accomplishment. Those attending the dinner party loved the savory shrimp over Gruyère-flavored grits. We prepared the sauce a couple of hours early and kept it warm until serving time. That way the shrimp didn't overcook in the hot sauce while guests arrived and enjoyed the hors d'oeuvres. Right before serving, we added the shrimp to the sauce to cook just until done.

Gruyère Grits (page 122)
3 tablespoons extra virgin olive oil
1½ cups chopped red bell pepper
1 large white onion, finely chopped
1 to 2 garlic cloves, minced
6 ounces andouille sausage, sliced
½ cup dry white wine
⅓ cup all-purpose flour
2¼ cups less-sodium chicken broth

⅓ cup heavy whipping cream
2 bay leaves
1 to 1½ teaspoons Creole seasoning (such as Tony Chachere's)
3 pounds unpeeled large raw shrimp, peeled and deveined
2 tablespoons chopped fresh flat-leaf parsley

Prepare Gruyère Grits; set aside, and keep warm.

While grits are cooking, heat oil in a large skillet over medium heat; add bell pepper, onion, and garlic, and sauté 2 minutes to soften. Add sausage, and cook 6 to 7 minutes or until browned, stirring often. Add wine, and cook until almost all liquid has evaporated.

Sprinkle flour over mixture in skillet, and cook 3 minutes, stirring constantly. (Flour will start to brown.) Gradually whisk in chicken broth and cream; add bay leaves and Creole seasoning.

Bring mixture to a simmer, and cook, uncovered, 7 minutes or until thick, stirring often. (Mixture may be cooked to this point, and then covered and kept warm until serving time.)

Just before serving, add shrimp to sauce, and cook 3 to 4 minutes or until shrimp turn pink, stirring often. Remove and discard bay leaves, and stir in parsley. Spoon shrimp and sauce over Gruyère Grits, and serve immediately. **Yield:** 8 to 10 servings.

Lime-Marinated Shrimp with Bean and Mango Salsa over Grilled Grits Cakes

4½ cups water

1½ teaspoons salt

1½ cups uncooked stone-ground grits

¾ cup (3 ounces) freshly shredded Parmesan cheese

¼ to ⅛ teaspoon garlic powder

Bean and Mango Salsa (at right)

½ cup extra virgin olive oil

¼ cup fresh lime juice

1 tablespoon honey

1 garlic clove, minced

½ teaspoon salt

½ teaspoon black pepper

1⅓ pounds unpeeled large raw shrimp, peeled and deveined

Olive oil-flavored cooking spray

Combine water, 1½ teaspoons salt, and grits in a large, heavy saucepan; bring to a boil, stirring constantly. Reduce heat; simmer, uncovered, 20 to 25 minutes or until grits are very thick, stirring often. Remove from heat; add Parmesan cheese and garlic powder, stirring until cheese melts. Spoon grits into an 11- x 7-inch baking pan lined with heavy-duty plastic wrap, spreading evenly; cool 15 minutes. Place a dry paper towel over grits; cover and chill 2 hours or until very firm. (Grits will be even firmer and easier to grill if chilled overnight).

Prepare Bean and Mango salsa; chill. Combine olive oil and next 5 ingredients in a shallow dish; add shrimp, stirring to coat. Cover; chill 1 to 2 hours.

After grits are very firm, preheat grill to 350° to 400° (medium-high). Remove grits to a cutting board; cut grits into desired shape. Coat tops and bottoms of grits cakes with cooking spray. Grill, covered with grill lid, on a grill rack coated with cooking spray over medium-high heat (350° to 400°) until lightly browned and thoroughly heated. Keep warm.

Remove shrimp from marinade, and thread onto skewers. Grill, covered with grill lid, over medium-high heat (350° to 400°) 3 to 4 minutes on each side or until shrimp turn pink. Combine shrimp with Bean and Mango Salsa; serve over grilled grits cakes. **Yield:** 4 servings.

Leigh (my daughter) originally created the Bean and Mango Salsa to serve over Grits Bruschetta (recipe on page 50). But in a brainstorming session for a unique shrimp and grits recipe, her culinary instincts inspired her to pair the salsa with lime-marinated shrimp to be served over grilled grits cakes. The result—an intriguing entrée for a summer cookout. Be sure that your grill rack is very clean before coating it with cooking spray and cooking the grits cakes—otherwise they'll tend to stick.

Bean and Mango Salsa

In a medium bowl, combine 1 cup canned black beans (rinsed and drained), 2 cups chopped tomato, ½ cup chopped green bell pepper, ½ cup chopped mango, 1 tablespoon minced fresh onion, 2 tablespoons fresh lime juice, 1 tablespoon olive oil, 2 teaspoons chopped fresh cilantro, ½ teaspoon garlic powder, ½ teaspoon salt, ¼ teaspoon ground black pepper, and ¼ teaspoon ground red pepper. Cover and chill 2 hours. Yield: 2½ cups.

Shrimp and Blue Grits with Bacon Vinaigrette

Clifton Holt, Chef & Owner, Little Savannah Restaurant and Bar,

Birmingham, Alabama

chef's recipe

Chef Holt creates a striking presentation when he serves sautéed shrimp and mushrooms over cooked blue grits and adds a unique twist with a tangy drizzle of bacon vinaigrette. For a more traditional look, you can use white or yellow grits instead. For another of Clif's creations using blue grits, turn to page 137 for his Blue Corn Grits and Chorizo Sausage Spoonbread Soufflé.

Bacon Vinaigrette

Cook ½ pound diced bacon in a sauté pan or large skillet over medium heat 8 to 10 minutes or until browned and crisp. Remove bacon, reserving about ⅓ cup drippings; keep drippings warm. Combine 1 diced shallot, ½ cup sherry vinegar, 2 teaspoons light brown sugar, and ¾ teaspoon Dijon mustard; macerate (let stand) 15 minutes. Whisk drippings into vinegar mixture; keep vinaigrette warm until ready to use. Yield: about 1 cup.

3½ cups cold bottled water
1 teaspoon kosher salt
1 cup uncooked organic stone-ground blue corn grits
¼ cup freshly grated Parmesan cheese
2 tablespoons heavy whipping cream
Dash of Tabasco sauce
Additional kosher salt to taste
¼ cup extra virgin olive oil, divided
½ (8-ounce) package fresh mushrooms, quartered

32 large raw shrimp (about 1¾ pounds), peeled and deveined, but leaving tails on
1 garlic clove, crushed
1 cup white wine
Fresh thyme leaves (about 1 tablespoon)
Fresh minced parsley (about 1 tablespoon)
Reserved cooked bacon (from vinaigrette)
Bacon Vinaigrette (at left)

Bring water and 1 teaspoon kosher salt to a boil in a medium, heavy saucepan; vigorously whisk in grits. Return to a boil; reduce heat to low, and simmer, uncovered, 20 minutes or until thick, stirring every few minutes. Remove from heat; add Parmesan cheese, cream, Tabasco sauce, and additional kosher salt to taste (about 1 teaspoon). Cover and keep warm.

While grits are cooking, heat 2 tablespoons oil in a large sauté pan or skillet over medium-high heat; add mushrooms, and cook about 5 minutes or until tender. Remove from pan, and set aside. Add remaining 2 tablespoons oil to pan, and heat; add shrimp, and sauté 1 minute. Add garlic, wine, and kosher salt to taste (about 1 teaspoon). Cook 2 to 3 more minutes or until shrimp are almost done, stirring occasionally. Add mushrooms, thyme, and parsley to shrimp mixture, and cook, stirring constantly, just until shrimp are done. Using a slotted spoon, spoon shrimp mixture over hot grits; sprinkle with bacon, and drizzle 1 to 2 tablespoons Bacon Vinaigrette over top of each serving. Serve immediately. **Yield:** 4 servings.

Asiago Grits

For superb flavor, stir freshly grated Asiago cheese into the grits to accompany the Garlic Shrimp with Edamame and Tomatoes on page 114.

This Asiago and grits combination is also tasty with Easy Pork Grillades on page 82, but you'll need more grits— just add 1½ cups uncooked grits to 6 cups water and 1½ teaspoons salt. When the grits are done, stir in ¾ cup grated Asiago cheese.

4   cups water
1   teaspoon salt
1   cup uncooked stone-ground speckled, yellow, or white grits

½   cup (2 ounces) freshly grated Asiago or Parmesan cheese

Bring water and salt to a boil in a medium, heavy saucepan; gradually whisk in grits. Reduce heat; simmer, uncovered, 20 to 25 minutes or until thick, stirring often. Remove from heat; add cheese, stirring until cheese melts. **Yield:** 4 servings.

Gruyère Grits

Melted Gruyere adds a rich nutty flavor and creamy texture to cooked grits. These Gruyere-laced grits are delightful under one of my favorite shrimp and grits recipes—Anniversary Shrimp and Grits on page 116.

I love experimenting with different cheeses in my grits and recently prepared mouthwatering grits with fontina cheese. They were creamy, full of flavor, and would be scrumptious paired with almost any recipe for shrimp and grits.

8   cups milk
1½   teaspoons salt
2   cups uncooked stone-ground white or yellow grits

2   cups (8 ounces) shredded Gruyère cheese
¼   cup butter
½   teaspoon black pepper

Combine milk and salt in a large, heavy saucepan; cook over medium-high heat just until mixture starts to boil. (Be careful not to let milk boil out of the pan as it comes to a boil—it can do so quickly.) Gradually whisk in grits. Reduce heat; simmer, uncovered, 20 to 25 minutes or until thick, stirring often. Remove from heat, and add cheese, butter, and pepper, stirring until cheese melts; cover and keep warm. **Yield:** 8 to 10 servings.

Green Onion Grits

½	tablespoon olive oil	4	cups water
1	cup sliced green onions	1	teaspoon salt
1	garlic clove, minced	1	cup uncooked stone-ground grits

Prepare these tasty grits to serve under my light version of Shrimp Creole on page 115.

Heat oil in a medium, heavy saucepan over medium-high heat. Add green onions and garlic; sauté 2 minutes. Add water and salt, and bring to a boil; gradually whisk in grits. Reduce heat; simmer, uncovered, 20 to 25 minutes or until thick, stirring often. **Yield:** 4 servings.

Simple Shrimp and Grits

3⅓	cups water	1	tablespoon olive oil
1	teaspoon salt	2	pounds unpeeled large raw shrimp, peeled and deveined
1	cup uncooked stone-ground grits	1	tablespoon Worcestershire sauce
⅔	cup whipping cream	2	teaspoons Creole seasoning
¾	cup (3 ounces) shredded Parmesan cheese	¼	teaspoon black pepper
½	teaspoon Creole seasoning		

Also known as College Shrimp and Grits in my home, this recipe was developed by my daughter when she lived in student apartments in Greenville, South Carolina. She created the recipe from a few ingredients in her tiny pantry and reports that her friends loved the flavorful shrimp combined with hearty grits.

Bring water and salt to a boil in a large, heavy saucepan; whisk in grits. Reduce heat; simmer, uncovered, 20 minutes, stirring often. Stir in cream; cook 5 to 10 minutes or until grits are thick and creamy. Remove from heat, and stir in cheese and ½ teaspoon Creole seasoning; cover and keep warm.

While grits are cooking, heat oil in a large nonstick skillet over medium-high heat. Add shrimp and next 3 ingredients. Sauté shrimp 4 to 5 minutes or until shrimp turn pink; drain. Add shrimp to grits mixture, stirring to combine; serve immediately. **Yield:** 4 to 6 servings.

Grits and polenta are such friendly foods—they don't have to take center stage and they're perfectly content to let other ingredients shine. That's what happens when creative cooks stir fresh herbs, spicy horseradish, or even truffles into creamy, cooked grits

side dishes

and polenta. And when a Southern chef combines chorizo sausage with cornmeal, grits, and eggs, the result is a delightfully seasoned side dish known as Blue Corn Grits and Chorizo Sausage Spoonbread Soufflé.

Anson Mills' Black Truffle Grits

Mark Hibbs, Chef & Owner, Ratcliffe On The Green,

Charlotte, North Carolina

chef's recipe

Chef Hibbs uses organic white stone-ground grits from Anson Mills in Columbia, South Carolina. He chooses Anson Mills because it's a certified organic gristmill that specializes in heirloom varieties of corn. Mark grants these grits a lot of respect by dressing them with black truffles. To maximize the flavor contribution of the truffles, he dices them into a brunoise-cut of small (⅛-inch) pieces and enhances their taste with black truffle oil. Mark's careful attention to culinary detail has certainly paid off: The James Beard Foundation has recognized him as one of the Southeast's best chefs.

truffles

Very rare and quite pricey, truffles contribute a unique pungency to contemporary cuisine. Fortunately, truffles are so potent that just a small amount goes a long way. Fresh imported truffles are available in the late fall and winter in many specialty food markets. Canned truffles, truffle paste in a tube, and truffle oil are also found in specialty stores.

Turn to page 13 to read a description of Chef Hibbs' popular grits dish as it appeared in Uptown Magazine.

4	cups 40% heavy cream (heavy whipping cream)		Kosher salt to taste
4	cups water		Black pepper to taste
2	cups uncooked Anson Mills organic white corn quick grits (see Note)	1	tablespoon brunoise-cut Perigord black truffle
		¼	cup black truffle oil

Combine cream and water in a large, heavy saucepan; cook over medium-high heat just until mixture starts to boil. Gradually whisk in grits; reduce heat to medium. Simmer, uncovered, 20 to 25 minutes or until grits are fully cooked, stirring often. Remove from heat, and add kosher salt to taste (about 4 teaspoons) and pepper to taste (about ½ teaspoon).

Add black truffle and truffle oil to grits, stirring to blend; cover and let stand 15 minutes. **Yield:** 8 (1-cup) servings.

Note: The length of time required for cooking grits depends on how finely the corn was ground. Most "quick" grits sold in the grocery store are done after simmering for about 5 minutes. However, the "quick" grits sold by Anson Mills are similar in texture to most regular, stone-ground grits and require 20 to 25 minutes of cook time. Anson Mills' coarsely ground grits require 50 minutes or more to cook. It's always best to follow the gristmill's package directions for appropriate cook time.

Creamy Horseradish Grits

A traditional accompaniment to roast beef is some form of potato, but I'm partial to a fresh, innovative companion—grits seasoned with horseradish.

3½ cups water

1¼ teaspoons salt

1 cup uncooked stone-ground grits

¼ cup sour cream

2 tablespoons prepared horseradish

⅛ teaspoon freshly ground black pepper

Bring water and salt to a boil in a medium, heavy saucepan; gradually whisk in grits. Reduce heat; simmer, uncovered, 20 to 25 minutes or until thick, stirring often. Remove from heat; add sour cream, horseradish, and pepper, stirring to blend. **Yield:** 4 servings.

Blue Cheese Grits

Blue cheese fans will adore these flavorful grits—especially when grilled steak is on your menu. For a fun splash of color on the plate, start with blue corn grits.

2½ cups water

¾ teaspoon salt

¾ cup uncooked stone-ground blue or white grits

¼ cup ricotta cheese

2 to 3 ounces crumbled blue cheese

¼ teaspoon black pepper

Bring water and salt to a boil in a medium, heavy saucepan; gradually whisk in grits. Reduce heat; simmer, uncovered, 20 to 25 minutes or until thick, stirring often. Remove from heat; add ricotta cheese, blue cheese, and pepper, stirring to blend. **Yield:** 4 servings.

Creamy Gruyère Grits Casserole

To celebrate the marriage of some of my children's friends, I have prepared many grits casseroles for engagement party buffets. We bake the casseroles a couple of hours early, and then cover the hot dishes with aluminum foil. One of my cooking companions, Kelley, taught me the secret to keeping the casseroles hot as they travel to the host house. We wrap each foil-covered casserole in a heavy towel, and then place the towel-wrapped dish into a large thermal ice chest. For a large dinner party, I've even stacked two or three casseroles in the chest, with a baking sheet or jelly-roll pan between them. Just as it keeps cold food cold, the chest retains heat and keeps hot food hot.

why organic?

Before a food can be labeled "organic," its grower and producer must adhere to strict guidelines from the U.S. Department of Agriculture (USDA) about how the farmer and processor grow and handle the food before it reaches restaurant chefs or cooks at home. Food experts often claim that organic products taste better—that's certainly the opinion of many chefs. And some researchers have reported that organic produce is richer in certain nutrients. But one of the most convincing arguments to buy organic is simply to avoid unnecessary pesticides, herbicides, and other chemicals.

6½ cups water
1½ teaspoons salt
2 cups uncooked stone-ground grits
½ cup heavy whipping cream
½ cup butter, divided
2 cups (8 ounces) shredded Gruyère cheese
½ teaspoon black pepper
¾ cup chopped green onions
2 garlic cloves, minced
2 large eggs, lightly beaten
Cooking spray
½ cup (2 ounces) freshly grated Parmesan cheese

Preheat oven to 350°. Bring water and salt to a boil in a large, heavy saucepan; gradually whisk in grits. Reduce heat; simmer, uncovered, 20 minutes, stirring often. Add cream, and cook 5 more minutes or until grits are thick and tender, stirring constantly. Remove from heat; add ¼ cup butter, Gruyère cheese, and pepper, stirring until butter and cheese melt.

While grits are cooking, melt remaining ¼ cup butter in a skillet; add green onions and garlic, and sauté 3 minutes. Add green onion mixture to cooked grits mixture; gradually add eggs, stirring to blend. Pour into a 13- x 9-inch baking dish coated with cooking spray; sprinkle with Parmesan cheese. Bake, uncovered, at 350° for 35 to 40 minutes or until set. **Yield:** 10 to 12 servings.

Garlic-and-Herb Grits Casserole

2   cups water
2   cups milk
¾   teaspoon salt
1   cup uncooked stone-ground grits
1   (4-ounce) container garlic-and-herb
     flavored spreadable cheese (such as
     Alouette)

½   cup (2 ounces) freshly grated
     Parmesan cheese
½   teaspoon black pepper
2   large eggs, lightly beaten
Cooking spray
Paprika

Grits casseroles are great make-ahead dishes. Just cook and season the grits, assemble the casserole, and chill the dish until an hour or so before serving time. Allow the dish to sit at room temperature for about 30 minutes before putting it in the oven. If the grits mixture is still very cold, you may need to bake the casserole a few extra minutes.

Preheat oven to 350°. Combine water, milk, and salt in a large, heavy saucepan; cook over medium-high heat just until mixture starts to boil. (Watch closely, as the milk mixture can boil out of the pan quickly.) Gradually whisk in grits. Reduce heat; simmer, uncovered, 20 to 25 minutes or until thick, stirring often. Remove from heat; whisk in cheeses and pepper.

Gradually whisk eggs into grits mixture. Pour grits mixture into an 11- x 7-inch baking dish coated with cooking spray; sprinkle with paprika. Bake, uncovered, at 350° for 40 minutes or until set. **Yield:** 6 to 8 servings.

Grits Alfredo

3⅔ cups water
¾   teaspoon salt
1   cup uncooked stone-ground grits
¼   cup heavy whipping cream

½   cup (2 ounces) shredded Parmesan
     or Asiago cheese
1   slice applewood smoked bacon,
     cooked and chopped

Pass on the pasta and instead stir traditional Alfredo ingredients into cooked grits for a side dish that the whole family will love.

Bring water and salt to a boil in a heavy saucepan; gradually whisk in grits. Reduce heat; simmer, uncovered, 20 minutes, stirring often. Add cream, and cook 5 minutes or until grits are thick and tender, stirring constantly. Remove from heat; add cheese and chopped bacon, stirring until cheese melts. **Yield:** 4 servings.

Grits Primavera

Turn this nutritious recipe into a colorful one-dish meal by adding chopped cooked chicken to the vegetable mixture.

4 cups water	1 cup matchstick carrots
1 teaspoon salt	1 cup julienne-cut green bell pepper
1 cup uncooked stone-ground yellow or white grits	1 cup julienne-cut zucchini or asparagus
¼ cup (1 ounce) freshly grated Parmesan cheese	1 cup sliced fresh mushrooms
3 tablespoons julienne-cut fresh basil	1 cup grape tomatoes, halved
1½ teaspoons extra virgin olive oil	½ cup refrigerated cooked edamame or frozen sweet peas, thawed
Cooking spray	1 (10-ounce) container light Alfredo sauce (such as Buitoni)
2 garlic cloves, minced	

Bring water and salt to a boil in a medium, heavy saucepan; gradually whisk in grits. Reduce heat; simmer, uncovered, 20 to 25 minutes or until thick, stirring often. Remove from heat; add cheese and basil, stirring until cheese melts. Cover and keep warm.

While grits are cooking, heat oil in a large skillet coated with cooking spray over medium-high heat; add garlic, and sauté 1 minute. Add carrots, bell pepper, and zucchini; sauté 3 minutes. Add mushrooms, tomatoes, and edamame; sauté 4 to 5 minutes. Remove vegetables from skillet.

Add Alfredo sauce to skillet, and cook over low heat, stirring constantly, until thoroughly heated (about 5 minutes). Return vegetables to skillet, and cook just until heated through. Serve vegetable mixture over hot cooked grits. **Yield:** 4 servings.

Mexican Spoonbread

Truly Southern in origin, spoonbread is a soufflélike dish with an ingredient list similar to cornbread. Because of its soft texture, spoonbread should be served with a spoon and is more of a side dish than a bread. This version calls for soaking the cornmeal in boiling water to tenderize the stone-ground grain. A word of advice: Be sure to serve spoonbread hot out of the oven to maximize its moistness.

1½ cups boiling water
1   cup stone-ground yellow cornmeal
¼   cup butter
½   teaspoon salt
2   large eggs, lightly beaten
1   cup buttermilk

1½ teaspoons baking powder
1   cup (4 ounces) shredded Monterey
    Jack cheese with jalapeño peppers
1   (11-ounce) can Mexican corn with
    red and green bell peppers, drained
Cooking spray

Preheat oven to 375°. Pour boiling water over cornmeal in a medium bowl, stirring until smooth and blended. Quickly add butter and salt, stirring until butter melts. Let mixture stand 10 minutes.

Combine eggs and buttermilk in a small bowl. Gradually add buttermilk mixture to cornmeal mixture. Whisk in baking powder until blended; stir in cheese and corn. Pour into an 11- x 7-inch baking dish coated with cooking spray. Bake, uncovered, at 375° for 40 to 45 minutes or until golden brown. Serve immediately. **Yield:** 6 servings.

Cracklin' Grits Spoonbread

Alan Martin, Executive Chef, Standard Bistro, Birmingham, Alabama

Cracklings are crispy pieces of rendered fat–usually from pork but sometimes from the skin of a duck. While Chef Martin prefers the light crispy texture and unmistakable flavor that cracklings contribute to his spoonbread, he recommends smoked bacon here since cracklings may be difficult to find. If you want to use cracklings instead of bacon, you'll need ⅓ cup.

3   cups water
1   teaspoon kosher salt
¾   cup uncooked stone-ground yellow grits
4   slices applewood smoked bacon
1½ cups finely ground yellow cornmeal
1½ teaspoons baking powder
Kosher salt to taste
Cracked black pepper to taste

¼   cup chopped scallions (green onions)
2   tablespoons diced seeded red chile pepper (such as red poblano)
2   large eggs, lightly beaten
2   cups whole milk
⅓   cup heavy whipping cream
Softened butter or cooking spray

Bring water and 1 teaspoon kosher salt to a boil; gradually whisk in grits. Reduce heat, and simmer, uncovered, 20 to 25 minutes or until thick, stirring often; keep warm. Cook bacon in a large, heavy skillet until crisp. Remove bacon from skillet, reserving 2 tablespoons drippings. Chop bacon.

Preheat oven to 375°. Combine cornmeal, baking powder, kosher salt to taste (about 1 teaspoon), and black pepper to taste (about ¼ teaspoon) in a bowl until well blended; add bacon, scallions, and diced red pepper. Whisk together eggs, milk, and cream in a second bowl; stir cooked grits into egg mixture. Whisk wet ingredients into dry ingredients; whisk in 2 tablespoons reserved hot bacon drippings. Grease 10 (6-ounce) ramekins with butter or coat with cooking spray. Divide batter evenly among ramekins. Bake at 375° for 25 minutes or until lightly browned. **Yield:** 10 servings.

chef's recipe

Chef Martin's menu, blending Southern cooking and French cuisine, features local organic produce from nearby Mt. Laurel Organic Gardens as well as free-range and organic meats, fowl, and lamb. Alan is also particular about his grits, insisting that stone-ground grits are definitely the best. He cautions that some mills sell stone-ground grits with excessive husks that should be removed before cooking. Alan explains, "To remove the husks, whisk the grits in cold water, and allow the husks to float to the top. Then skim off the husks with a strainer." He also advises, "All grits, polenta, and cornmeal are different. Some are more coarse and some more fine. Adjust your recipes according to the product you are using. When using extra fine meal, use more liquid. When using coarse meal or grits, use less liquid."

Southern Cornbread Dressing

Don't wait until Thanksgiving to enjoy this delicacy—prepare it to serve along-side roasted or grilled chicken or pork. If you're using leftover cornbread and biscuits, you'll need about 3 cups cornbread crumbs and 2 cups biscuit crumbs.

Old-Fashioned Buttermilk Cornbread
    for an 8-inch skillet (page 60)
Buttermilk Biscuits
2 tablespoons butter
½ cup chopped red bell pepper
½ cup chopped onion
½ cup chopped celery

1 cup turkey or chicken broth
½ cup whole milk
1 large egg, lightly beaten
1 teaspoon poultry seasoning
½ teaspoon rubbed sage
¼ teaspoon black pepper
Cooking spray

Prepare Old-Fashioned Buttermilk Cornbread and Buttermilk Biscuits; cool to touch. Coarsely crumble cornbread and biscuits. Place crumbs in a large bowl, and set aside. Reduce oven temperature to 350°.

Melt butter in a heavy skillet; add bell pepper, onion, and celery, and cook over medium-high heat until tender, stirring often. Add vegetables to crumbs in bowl. Combine broth and next 5 ingredients. Pour over crumb mixture, and toss gently to mix. Spoon mixture into an 8-inch square baking dish coated with cooking spray; press down lightly to even out mixture. Bake dressing, uncovered, at 350° for 40 to 45 minutes or until lightly browned. Let stand 10 minutes before serving. **Yield:** 6 to 8 servings.

Buttermilk Biscuits

3 tablespoons cold butter,
    cut into small pieces

1 cup soft-wheat self-rising flour
    (such as White Lily)
¼ cup plus 2 tablespoons buttermilk

Preheat oven to 425°. Cut butter into flour with a pastry blender until mixture is crumbly. Sprinkle with buttermilk, and stir just until dry ingredients

cornbread dressing muffins:
Prepare Southern Cornbread Dressing mixture as directed at right for 6 to 8 servings. Spoon mixture into 2½-inch muffin cups coated with cooking spray; bake at 375° for 35 minutes or until lightly browned. Let muffins stand 10 minutes before removing from pans. Yield: 1 dozen.

are moistened. Turn dough out onto a lightly floured surface, and knead 3 or 4 times. Roll to about ¾-inch thickness. Cut with a 2½-inch biscuit cutter, and place on a lightly greased baking sheet. Bake at 425° for 12 to 15 minutes or until lightly browned. **Yield:** 4 biscuits.

cornbread dressing for a crowd:
Double ingredients for Southern Cornbread Dressing on previous page, and spoon into a 13- x 9-inch baking dish coated with cooking spray. Bake at 350° for 50 minutes or until lightly browned. Yield: 12 servings.

Sausage and Grits Dressing

pictured on page 124

My friend and mentor, Kathy Eakin, introduced me to this unique twist on Southern-style dressing that she prepares for holiday dinners at her family home in Shelbyville, Tennessee. The recipe first appeared in Christmas with Southern Living® 2001.

2 (10½-ounce) cans condensed chicken broth, undiluted
1¼ cups water
1¼ cups uncooked stone-ground white or yellow grits
1 cup (4 ounces) freshly shredded Parmesan cheese
Cooking spray
1 pound ground hot pork sausage
⅓ cup butter
5 celery ribs with leaves, finely chopped
4 garlic cloves, minced (about 1 tablespoon)
1 large onion, chopped
½ cup chopped fresh parsley
1 large egg, lightly beaten

Combine broth, water, and grits in a large, heavy saucepan; bring to a boil, stirring constantly. Reduce heat, and simmer, uncovered, 20 to 25 minutes or until very thick, stirring often. Remove from heat, and add Parmesan cheese, stirring to melt cheese. Spoon grits mixture into a 13- x 9-inch baking pan lined with heavy-duty plastic wrap or coated with cooking spray. Cool completely. Cover and chill grits 2 hours or until very firm.

Preheat oven to 450°. Invert grits onto a large cutting board, and remove plastic wrap. Cut grits into ¾-inch cubes. Place in a single layer on a large baking sheet or jelly-roll pan coated with cooking spray. Bake at 450° for 20 minutes; turn grits cubes, and bake 12 more minutes or until crisp and browned. Reduce oven temperature to 350°.

Cook sausage in a large skillet, stirring to crumble, until sausage is no longer pink; remove sausage from skillet, reserving drippings in skillet. Add butter to drippings in skillet, and place over medium-high heat until butter melts. Add celery, garlic, and onion; sauté 5 minutes or until vegetables are tender. Combine onion mixture, sausage, grits cubes, and parsley, tossing gently. Drizzle egg over grits mixture, and toss gently; spoon into an 11- x 7-inch baking dish coated with cooking spray. Bake, uncovered, at 350° for 40 to 45 minutes or until browned. **Yield:** 8 servings.

Blue Corn Grits and Chorizo Sausage Spoonbread Soufflé

Clifton Holt, Chef & Owner, Little Savannah Restaurant and Bar,

Birmingham, Alabama

Chef Holt and wife, Maureen, offer true Southern hospitality to guests at their neighborhood restaurant in the historic Forest Park community of Birmingham, Alabama. Clif's goal is to feature products from local purveyors such as the Jones Valley Urban Farm, the farm at Snow's Bend, and the McEwens' nearby gristmill. The Holts say that "knowing where our food comes from is a priority for our restaurant." Maureen even tends a garden behind the restaurant that provides fresh vegetables and herbs.

1½ pounds chorizo sausage

4 cups milk

½ cup plus 2 tablespoons uncooked stone-ground blue grits

2 tablespoons unsalted butter

2 teaspoons kosher salt

6 large eggs, separated

1 tablespoon baking powder

Additional unsalted butter

chef's recipe

Chef Holt likes to prepare and serve blue grits in his restaurant and he even prepared blue grits to accompany marinated quail when invited to cook at the prestigious James Beard House in New York City. When asked why he's so fond of grits, Clif says, "Grits, however prepared, seem to ease people and bring about comfort in their Southernness."

Preheat oven to 350°. Cook sausage in a large, heavy skillet 10 to 12 minutes or until browned, stirring to crumble. Drain excess fat.

Cook milk in a heavy saucepan until scalded (do not allow to boil). Whisk in grits, and cook over medium heat, whisking constantly, 15 minutes or until mixture is like a thick mush. Add 2 tablespoons butter and salt to grits, stirring to melt butter. In a separate bowl, combine egg yolks and baking powder, stirring to blend; gradually add yolk mixture to cooked grits. Stir in crumbled sausage. Beat egg whites at high speed with an electric mixer until stiff (but not dry and grainy). Fold beaten egg whites into grits mixture.

Grease a 13- x 9-inch baking dish or 3-quart soufflé dish with additional butter. Pour grits mixture into dish; bake, uncovered, at 350° for 30 to 40 minutes or until lightly browned. (Cooking time will vary depending on the type of baking dish used.) Serve immediately. **Yield:** 6 to 8 servings.

Parmesan Polenta with Artichokes and Pesto

You can have this easy polenta dish ready in under 20 minutes. Adding artichoke hearts and pesto creates a distinctive and flavorful side dish to accompany the Eggplant Parmesan on page 101.

4 cups water

½ teaspoon salt

1 cup uncooked stone-ground yellow polenta

1 cup drained marinated artichoke hearts

½ cup (2 ounces) freshly shredded Parmesan cheese

¼ cup commercial pesto

Fresh basil or freshly shaved Parmesan cheese (optional)

Bring water and salt to a boil in a medium, heavy saucepan; gradually whisk in polenta. Reduce heat; simmer, uncovered, 12 to 14 minutes or until thick and smooth, stirring often.

Coarsely chop ½ cup artichoke hearts; slice remaining artichoke hearts lengthwise into quarters.

Remove polenta from heat; add ½ cup Parmesan cheese, stirring to melt cheese. Add pesto and artichokes, stirring gently. Garnish with fresh basil or shaved Parmesan, if desired. Serve immediately. **Yield:** 6 servings.

Sweet Corn Polenta Pudding

Combine the sweet taste of summer corn with smooth polenta and thyme in this easy, spoonbreadlike casserole. It's best with fresh thyme, but don't hesitate to use dried if fresh isn't available.

2	tablespoons olive oil	1	teaspoon baking powder
½	cup finely chopped onion	¾	teaspoon salt
3	cups fresh corn kernels (about 5 ears)	½	teaspoon black pepper
		2	large eggs, lightly beaten
1	teaspoon fresh thyme leaves or about ¼ teaspoon dried thyme	1⅓	cups milk
		2	(1.5-ounce) slices hearty white bread
½	cup uncooked stone-ground polenta		Cooking spray

Preheat oven to 325°. Heat oil in a large, heavy skillet over medium-high heat; add onion, and sauté 3 minutes. Add corn and thyme; cook 4 minutes, stirring constantly.

Combine polenta, baking powder, salt, and pepper in a large bowl; add eggs, milk, and corn mixture, stirring to blend. Remove crusts from bread, and discard; cut bread into cubes. Add bread to polenta mixture, and toss to combine. Pour mixture into an 8-inch square baking dish coated with cooking spray. Bake, uncovered, at 325° for 30 to 35 minutes or until set. **Yield:** 6 to 8 servings.

summer corn

A culinary highlight of summer in the South is the availability of flavorful fresh corn. I love to eat corn straight from the cob after it's cooked briefly in boiling water and seasoned with melted butter. But fresh summer corn is also delicious in recipes like Sweet Corn Polenta Pudding. Fresh corn tastes best right after it's picked, when the corn's natural sweetness is at its peak.

Colorful Polenta

Red, yellow, and green vegetables make this polenta a pleasing side dish for grilled chicken or fish.

polenta

Just as potatoes are standard side-dish fare in the United States, polenta accompanies many meals in Northern Italy. Talented cooks serve polenta in a wide variety of ways, from the simplest seasoning of melted butter to the addition of rich cheeses, like Parmigiano-Reggiano. Like grits, seasoned cooked polenta can be poured into a pan, chilled until firm, and cut into cakes to be baked, broiled, grilled, or panfried.

4   cups water
2   teaspoons chicken-flavored bouillon granules
1   cup uncooked stone-ground yellow or white polenta
1   tablespoon butter
½   cup chopped red bell pepper
1   cup fresh or frozen whole kernel corn, thawed
½   cup chopped green onions
½   teaspoon salt
¼   teaspoon black pepper

Bring water and bouillon granules to a boil in a large, heavy saucepan over high heat; gradually whisk in polenta until smooth. Reduce heat, and simmer, uncovered, 12 to 14 minutes or until thick and creamy, stirring often.

While polenta is cooking, melt butter in a skillet over medium-high heat. Add red bell pepper, and cook 3 minutes, stirring often. Add corn and green onions; cook 2 minutes, stirring often.

Stir corn mixture, salt, and black pepper into cooked polenta. **Yield:** 6 servings.

Panko- and Cornmeal-Fried Okra

1 cup stone-ground cornmeal
⅔ cup panko (Japanese breadcrumbs)
1¼ teaspoons salt
1 teaspoon black pepper

¾ pound okra, cut into ½-inch slices
1 cup buttermilk
Vegetable oil

Combine first 4 ingredients in a zip-top plastic bag. Dip okra, in batches, into buttermilk; place okra in bag with cornmeal mixture. Shake to coat.

Pour vegetable oil to a depth of 1 inch in a Dutch oven or deep cast-iron skillet; heat to 375°. Fry okra, in batches, 2 minutes or until golden brown, turning if needed. Drain on a wire rack over paper towels. **Yield:** 4 to 6 servings.

the crunchiest fried okra
Lots of chefs and home cooks are using crispy Japanese breadcrumbs, called panko, to add crunch to their fried foods. Panko browns quite well and stays remarkably crisp, but I can't imagine panko replacing cornmeal for Southern fried okra. Panko- and Cornmeal-Fried Okra combines the two ingredients to get the best of both—the classic corn flavor of cornmeal along with the light, extra crispy crunch of panko.

Creole Fried Green Tomatoes

1 large egg, lightly beaten
¾ cup buttermilk
1 cup stone-ground cornmeal
1½ teaspoons Creole seasoning

3 green tomatoes, cut into ⅓-inch slices
All-purpose flour
Vegetable oil

Combine egg and buttermilk in a shallow bowl. Combine cornmeal and Creole seasoning in a separate shallow bowl, mixing well. Dip tomato slices in buttermilk mixture. Dredge each tomato slice in flour, dip again in buttermilk mixture, and dredge in cornmeal mixture to coat.

Pour oil to a depth of ½ inch in a large cast-iron skillet; heat over medium-high heat until hot. Carefully add tomato slices, in batches, in a single layer in skillet; cook 2 minutes on each side or until lightly browned. Remove from skillet, and drain on a wire rack over paper towels. Repeat procedure with remaining tomato slices. Serve immediately. **Yield:** 4 to 6 servings.

When summer approaches and the weather begins to warm, Southerners crave this classic vegetable side dish—fried green tomatoes. We pick green tomatoes before they have a chance to ripen on the vine, and then dredge the tomato slices in seasoned stone-ground cornmeal to create the crispy outer coating.

Even desserts deserve attention to texture as well as taste. Culinary connoisseurs are turning to cornmeal and polenta to add a hint of desirable crunchiness to cakes, cookies, cobblers, puddings, and pastries. You may already use cornmeal in a

desserts

chess pie, but have you ever considered a sweet bread pudding that starts with cornbread? Even the South's favorite pecan pie benefits from a cornmeal crust and the surprising addition of grits to the filling.

Strawberry Cornmeal Shortcakes

One of my favorite springtime desserts is strawberry shortcake, made with sweetened biscuits, fresh strawberries, and whipped cream. Adding cornmeal to the biscuit dough gives this old-fashioned dessert a pleasing new texture.

1   (16-ounce) carton fresh strawberries, sliced (about 3 cups)
7   tablespoons granulated sugar, divided
1   cup all-purpose flour
⅓   cup finely ground or sifted stone-ground white cornmeal (see page 23)
2   teaspoons baking powder
6   tablespoons cold butter, cut into small pieces
1   large egg, lightly beaten
½   cup sour cream
½   teaspoon vanilla extract
Cooking spray
1   to 2 teaspoons turbinado sugar
½   cup heavy whipping cream

Preheat oven to 425°. Combine strawberries and 4 tablespoons granulated sugar in a bowl, and toss to coat. Cover and set aside.

In a separate bowl, combine flour, cornmeal, 2 tablespoons granulated sugar, and baking powder until well blended; cut in butter with a pastry blender or fingertips until mixture is crumbly.

Whisk together egg, sour cream, and vanilla until blended; add to flour mixture, stirring just until dry ingredients are moistened. Coat a ⅓-cup measure with cooking spray; use measure to drop dough into 5 mounds onto a baking sheet lined with parchment paper. Sprinkle dough with turbinado sugar. Bake at 425° for 11 to 12 minutes or until golden brown.

Beat whipping cream at medium speed with an electric mixer until foamy; increase speed to high, and gradually add 1 tablespoon granulated sugar, beating until stiff peaks form. Split shortcakes in half horizontally. Spoon whipped cream evenly on bottom halves. Spoon ⅓ to ½ cup strawberry mixture onto whipped cream on each shortcake bottom; top with shortcake tops. Serve immediately. **Yield:** 5 servings.

a nutritious look at dessert

As a registered dietitian and calorie-counter for many years, I'm quite aware of what mouthwatering desserts can do to one's best intentions to eat healthy. But the truth is—I just can't give up my sweets! So one of my goals with desserts is to add nutrients wherever possible. Stone-ground cornmeal is one way to boost whole-grain goodness. And, of course, fiber-rich fruits, such as ripe, juicy strawberries, contribute natural sweetness as well as valuable vitamins and minerals.

Cinnamon-Blueberry Coffee Cake

This easy coffee cake gets a nutrient boost from fresh blueberries stirred into the batter. You'll be tempted to cut into the mouthwatering cake right after it comes out of the oven, but you can slice it more neatly after it cools completely.

cornmeal for dessert recipes

Stone-ground cornmeal from some gristmills may contain more large grains and flecks of husks than you'd like for some recipes, especially desserts. Buying finely ground cornmeal (sometimes called "bolted cornmeal") may solve this dilemma, or you can gently sift the cornmeal through a wire strainer to remove some of those large pieces before measuring the meal.

⅓ cup firmly packed light brown sugar
⅓ cup chopped walnuts
1 teaspoon ground cinnamon
1 cup butter, softened
2 cups granulated sugar
2 large eggs
1 cup sour cream
1 teaspoon vanilla extract

1¼ cups all-purpose flour
½ cup finely ground or sifted stone-ground cornmeal (see page 23)
1½ teaspoons baking powder
½ teaspoon salt
1 cup fresh blueberries
Cooking spray

Preheat oven to 350°. Combine brown sugar, walnuts, and cinnamon in a small bowl; set aside.

Beat butter at medium speed with an electric mixer until creamy; gradually add granulated sugar, beating until light and fluffy. Add eggs, 1 at a time, beating just until yellow disappears. Stir in sour cream and vanilla. Combine flour and next 3 ingredients in a bowl until well blended. Gradually add to butter mixture, beating just until blended. Fold in blueberries.

Spoon half of batter into an 8-inch square pan coated with cooking spray; sprinkle half of walnut mixture atop batter in pan. Repeat procedure with remaining batter and walnut mixture. Bake at 350° for 1 hour to 1 hour and 10 minutes or until a wooden pick inserted in center comes out clean. Cool in pan. **Yield:** 12 servings.

Orange-Cornmeal Pound Cake with Cranberry-Port Sauce

Southern favorite

pictured on page 144

Cornmeal adds distinctive texture to this orange-kissed pound cake. I love it dressed up with the elegant Cranberry-Port Sauce, but it's equally yummy with vanilla ice cream or a glass of cold milk.

1   cup butter, softened
1   (8-ounce) package cream cheese, softened
2¾ cups sugar
6   large eggs
1¾ cups all-purpose flour
1   cup finely ground or sifted stone-ground yellow or white cornmeal (see page 23)
½   teaspoon baking powder
⅛   teaspoon salt
2   teaspoons grated orange rind
1½ teaspoons vanilla extract
Cooking spray for baking
Cranberry-Port Sauce (at right)

Preheat oven to 325°. Beat butter and cream cheese at medium speed with an electric mixer until creamy; gradually add sugar, beating well. Add eggs, 1 at a time, beating after each addition. In a separate bowl, combine flour, cornmeal, baking powder, and salt until well blended; add to creamed mixture, beating just until blended. Stir in orange rind and vanilla.

Spoon batter into a 10-inch tube pan coated with cooking spray for baking (or grease and flour the pan). Bake at 325° for 1 hour and 10 minutes to 1 hour and 15 minutes or until a wooden pick inserted in center comes out clean. Remove from oven, and let stand 10 minutes. Remove from pan, and cool completely on a wire rack. Slice cake, and serve with Cranberry-Port Sauce. Or, if desired, cut the cake into cubes, and place in martini glasses; spoon Cranberry-Port Sauce over cake. **Yield:** 12 servings.

cranberry-port sauce:
Combine 1 cup sugar, 1 cup diced peeled pear, 1 cup ruby port, 1 (12-ounce) package fresh or frozen cranberries, and ¾ cup water in a saucepan; bring to a boil over medium-high heat, and cook 5 minutes, stirring constantly. Reduce heat to medium-low, and simmer about 10 minutes or until berries pop. Serve at room temperature over cake. Yield: about 3 cups.

Pineapple-Cranberry Upside-Down Cornbread Cake

¼   cup unsalted butter
¾   cup firmly packed light brown sugar
1   (15-ounce) can sliced pineapple in juice, undrained
⅓   cup sweetened dried cranberries
½   cup unsalted butter, softened
¾   cup granulated sugar
2   large eggs

1   cup all-purpose flour
1   cup finely ground or sifted stone-ground yellow or white cornmeal (see page 23)
2   teaspoons baking powder
¼   teaspoon salt
⅔   cup milk
1   teaspoon vanilla extract

Use a large cast-iron skillet for this old-fashioned dessert. It traditionally calls for placing colorful maraschino cherries into the centers of the pineapple rings, but I like the tangy flavor from the dried cranberries instead.

Preheat oven to 350°. Melt ¼ cup butter in a 10-inch cast-iron skillet over medium heat. (If skillet is not well seasoned, coat first with cooking spray.) Add brown sugar to melted butter in skillet, and cook about 2 minutes, stirring constantly. Remove skillet from heat, and spread mixture evenly in skillet. Remove 7 slices pineapple from can, and drain on paper towels. Reserve remaining pineapple and juice for another use. Place 1 pineapple slice on top of brown sugar mixture in center of skillet. Place remaining pineapple slices evenly around edges of skillet. Place cranberries in centers of pineapple slices and between pineapple slices; set aside.

Beat ½ cup butter at medium speed with an electric mixer until creamy; gradually add granulated sugar, beating well. Add eggs, 1 at a time, beating after each addition. In a separate bowl, combine flour, cornmeal, baking powder, and salt until well blended; add to egg mixture alternately with milk, beginning and ending with flour mixture. Beat at low speed until blended after each addition. Stir in vanilla, beating until blended. Carefully pour mixture over pineapple slices in skillet; bake at 350° for 40 to 45 minutes. Remove from oven; cool in skillet 30 minutes. Carefully invert skillet onto a serving platter, scraping any remaining sauce from skillet onto cake. Cut into wedges to serve. **Yield:** 8 to 10 servings.

Cornmeal Spice Cookies

I've always loved to bake cookies, and through the years have learned to appreciate parchment paper—it eliminates the need to grease baking sheets and also results in more evenly baked cookies. Since chilled cookie dough is often easier to handle, work with half of this dough at a time, leaving the other portion chilled.

½ cup shortening

½ cup butter, softened

½ cup granulated sugar

½ cup firmly packed dark brown sugar

1 large egg

¼ cup molasses

1½ cups all-purpose flour

⅔ cup finely ground or sifted stone-ground cornmeal (see page 23)

1½ teaspoons baking soda

1 teaspoon ground cinnamon

1 teaspoon ground ginger

½ teaspoon ground allspice

¼ teaspoon ground cloves

¼ teaspoon salt

Additional granulated sugar

Beat shortening, butter, and sugars at medium speed with an electric mixture until creamy; add egg and molasses, beating until blended. Combine flour and next 7 ingredients in a bowl until well blended. Gradually add flour mixture to shortening mixture, beating until blended. Cover and chill dough 1 hour.

Preheat oven to 350°. Shape dough into 1-inch balls, and roll in additional granulated sugar. Place on baking sheets lined with parchment paper; bake at 350° for 9 to 10 minutes. Cool on baking sheets 5 minutes; remove to wire racks to cool completely. **Yield:** about 4½ dozen.

Lemon Bars

Cornmeal adds an extra layer of crunch to the flaky pastry of this Southern tea time favorite.

Cooking spray
1¾ cups all-purpose flour, divided
1   cup finely ground or sifted stone-ground cornmeal (see page 23)
⅔ cup powdered sugar
¾ cup cold butter, cut into small pieces
1   teaspoon baking powder

4   large eggs, lightly beaten
1½ cups granulated sugar
2   teaspoons grated lemon rind
⅓ cup fresh lemon juice (about 2 lemons)
Additional powdered sugar

Preheat oven to 350°. Line a 13- x 9-inch pan with parchment paper, and coat with cooking spray. Combine 1¼ cups flour, cornmeal, and ⅔ cup powdered sugar; cut in butter with a pastry blender or fingertips until mixture is crumbly. Press cornmeal mixture into bottom of pan; bake at 350° for 18 minutes or until crust just starts to brown.

Meanwhile, combine remaining ½ cup flour and baking powder in a bowl. In a separate bowl, combine eggs, granulated sugar, lemon rind, and lemon juice, stirring to blend. Gradually whisk dry ingredients into egg mixture, stirring well. While crust is still warm, pour lemon mixture evenly over crust, and return to oven. Bake at 350° for 18 to 20 minutes or until lemon mixture is lightly browned and set. Remove from oven, and cool on a wire rack. Cover and chill thoroughly before slicing into squares. Dust lightly with additional powdered sugar. **Yield:** 4 dozen bars.

citrus success

The flavors of citrus and cornmeal blend nicely in several desserts—these cornmeal-enriched Lemon Bars, Lime Chess Pie with Coconut Cornmeal Crust (page 156), and Orange-Cornmeal Pound Cake with Cranberry-Port Sauce (page 149). When grating rind, be sure to grate just the outer zest of the lemon, orange, or lime, avoiding the bitter white pith underneath. And if you need fresh juice, first roll the fruit on the countertop with the palm of your hand before slicing it—you'll find it easier to squeeze, resulting in more juice. Microwaving the fruit whole for just a few seconds before slicing also makes juicing easier.

Raspberry-Cornmeal Thumbprint Cookies

I filled the thumbprint holes with raspberry jam for the photograph, but blackberry is also a delightful choice. I may even try orange marmalade the next time I bake these shapely and scrumptious cookies.

1   cup butter, softened
⅔   cup granulated sugar
½   teaspoon almond extract
1½ cups all-purpose flour
⅔   cup finely ground or sifted stone-ground white cornmeal (see page 23)

⅓   cup seedless raspberry or blackberry jam
1   cup powdered sugar
1½ teaspoons almond extract
2   to 3 teaspoons water

Preheat oven to 350°. Beat butter at medium speed with an electric mixer until creamy; gradually add granulated sugar, beating well. Add ½ teaspoon almond extract. Combine flour and cornmeal; gradually add to butter mixture, beating at low speed until mixture is blended and forms a ball.

Shape dough into 1¼-inch balls, and place 2 inches apart on baking sheets lined with parchment paper. Press thumb into each cookie to make an indentation. Fill center of each cookie with a rounded ¼ teaspoon jam. Bake at 350° for 12 to 13 minutes or until edges just begin to brown. Cool 1 to 2 minutes on baking sheets; remove to wire racks to cool completely.

Combine powdered sugar, 1½ teaspoons almond extract, and water, stirring to make a thin glaze. Place glaze in a small zip-top plastic freezer bag, and snip off 1 tiny corner of bag; squeeze bag to drizzle glaze over cookies. **Yield:** 3 dozen.

Lime Chess Pie with
Coconut Cornmeal Crust

Simple and classic, chess pie has been a favorite Southern dessert for generations. Original recipes called for basic ingredients of eggs, sugar, butter, and cornmeal, often with a splash of vinegar for tartness. My preference is to add lime or lemon juice instead. After trying this combination of lime in the filling and coconut in the crust, I've added chess pie to my list of favorite desserts.

Coconut Cornmeal Crust

4   large eggs

1½ cups sugar

Pinch of salt

¼   cup heavy whipping cream

1   tablespoon grated lime rind

¼   cup fresh lime juice

¼   cup butter, melted

3   tablespoons finely ground or sifted stone-ground cornmeal (see page 23)

2   tablespoons sweetened flaked coconut

Preheat oven to 400°. Prepare Coconut Cornmeal Crust, and bake at 400° for 6 minutes. Remove from oven, and reduce oven temperature to 325°.

While crust is baking, combine eggs, sugar, and salt in a mixing bowl; beat at medium speed with an electric mixer until thick and lemon-colored. Add cream and next 4 ingredients, beating until blended. Pour egg mixture into warm prebaked crust; sprinkle top with coconut. Bake at 325° for 40 minutes or until set. Serve pie warm or at room temperature. **Yield:** 8 servings.

Coconut Cornmeal Crust

1¼ cups all-purpose flour

¼   cup finely ground or sifted stone-ground cornmeal (see page 23)

1   tablespoon sugar

½   teaspoon salt

⅓   cup sweetened flaked coconut

¼   cup cold shortening

2   tablespoons cold butter

5   tablespoons buttermilk

Process flour, cornmeal, sugar, salt, and coconut in a food processor until well blended. Add shortening and butter to processor bowl; process 10 seconds or until mixture is crumbly. Add buttermilk, and pulse 6 times or until dry ingredients are moistened. Turn dough out onto a lightly floured surface, and shape into a ball. Using a floured rolling pin, roll pastry to ⅛-inch thickness on a lightly floured surface (12- to 13-inch diameter). Place in a 9-inch pie plate; fold edges under, and crimp. **Yield:** 1 piecrust.

Pecan-Grits Pie

pictured on page 2

1 cup water
¼ cup uncooked stone-ground
   yellow grits
¼ teaspoon salt
¼ cup plus 2 tablespoons butter
1 cup sugar

¾ cup corn syrup
3 large eggs, lightly beaten
2 teaspoons vanilla extract
1½ cups broken pecan halves, divided
Single-Crust Version of Buttermilk
   Cornmeal Crust (page 160)

Combine water and grits in a small saucepan; stir and let stand 1 minute. Carefully remove husks floating on top of water, using a small strainer. Add salt to grits; place over high heat, and bring to a boil, stirring constantly. Cover, reduce heat, and simmer 20 minutes or until thick, stirring often. (When cooking this small amount of grits, cover pan to avoid losing too much liquid as steam during cooking.) Cover and set aside.

Melt butter in a small saucepan; add sugar and corn syrup, and cook over medium-low heat about 10 minutes or until sugar dissolves, stirring constantly. Remove from heat. Whisk cooked grits into butter mixture; cool slightly. Whisk eggs and vanilla into butter mixture until blended.

Preheat oven to 325°. Place 1 cup broken pecan halves in bottom of unbaked Buttermilk Cornmeal Crust. Pour grits mixture over pecans in piecrust. Sprinkle with additional ½ cup pecans, and stir pecans very gently to coat with syrup and distribute evenly. Bake at 325° for 45 minutes or until set. (Shield edges of crust with aluminum foil after about 30 minutes to prevent excessive browning, if needed.) **Yield:** 8 servings.

Whenever our extended family gathers for a holiday dinner, I'm expected to prepare the pecan pie. That's because I love to put grits in the South's favorite pie! The sweetened grits-enhanced filling adds a hint of texture and makes a perfect pecan pie. You can use a store-bought pastry shell in a pinch, but I think it tastes much better in the Buttermilk Cornmeal Crust (page 160).

McIntosh Apple Pie

I prefer McIntosh apples for this family-favorite apple pie—hence the title. The recipe was actually inspired by my daddy's sister, Aunt Frankie McEwen, who has baked many mouthwatering pies and cakes in her 80-plus years.

¾ cup water

⅛ teaspoon salt

¼ cup uncooked stone-ground polenta

2 tablespoons butter

1 cup sugar

3 tablespoons all-purpose flour

¾ teaspoon ground cinnamon

1 teaspoon vanilla extract

2½ pounds McIntosh or other
    cooking apples (about 9 small)

Double-Crust Version of Buttermilk
    Cornmeal Crust (page 160)

Additional sugar

Bring water and salt to a boil in a small, heavy saucepan; gradually whisk in polenta. Reduce heat, and simmer 12 minutes, stirring constantly. (Polenta will be very thick.) Add butter, stirring to melt; stir in 1 cup sugar, flour, cinnamon, and vanilla.

Peel and core apples; cut into ¼-inch slices, and place in a large bowl. Add polenta mixture to apples, and toss to coat.

Preheat oven to 425°. Transfer apple mixture to unbaked bottom pie crust. Roll remaining pastry to ¼-inch thickness; transfer to top of pie. Trim off excess pastry along edges. Fold edges under, and crimp. Cut slits in top of crust for steam to escape; sprinkle with additional sugar. Bake at 425° for 10 minutes; reduce oven temperature to 350°, and bake 45 more minutes or until crust is lightly browned. (Shield edges of crust with aluminum foil after 15 minutes to prevent excessive browning, if needed.) **Yield:** 8 servings.

perfect apples

I love snacking on apples because they're refreshing, filling, easy-to-eat, and loaded with healthy fiber. While I keep a supply of Gala apples on hand for an afternoon snack, I prefer to make apple pie with McIntosh apples because they're sweet, have just the right amount of tanginess, and develop a tender consistency during baking. If McIntosh apples aren't available, Granny Smith, Braeburn, and Cortland apples are also great for pies—you can even use a combination.

Buttermilk Cornmeal Crust

(single crust)

Use this delicious crust with pecan, pumpkin, or apple pies—it has a delicate texture and browns nicely. Most cookbooks recommend a pastry blender for cutting shortening and/or butter into the flour mixture. Maybe because it's what Mother did—but I prefer to use my fingers to cut in the shortening. I usually remember the "proper method" and pick up a pastry blender to cut in the chunks of butter, but always go back to my fingers to make sure the mixture feels just right.

1¼ cups all-purpose flour
¼ cup finely ground or sifted stone-ground cornmeal (see page 23)
1 tablespoon sugar
½ teaspoon salt
¼ cup cold shortening
¼ cup cold butter, cut into pieces
4 to 5 tablespoons buttermilk

Combine first 4 ingredients in a bowl; cut in shortening and butter with a pastry blender or fingertips until mixture is about the size of small peas. Sprinkle buttermilk evenly over surface; stir with a fork just until dry ingredients are moistened. Cover and chill 1 hour, if desired. Roll pastry to ⅛-inch thickness on a lightly floured surface (about 12-inch diameter). Place in a 9-inch pie plate; fold edges under, and crimp. **Yield:** 1 pastry.

Buttermilk Cornmeal Crust

(double crust)

This version is a little sweeter—the extra sugar makes the top crust a little more flaky and tender.

2½ cups all-purpose flour
½ cup finely ground or sifted stone-ground cornmeal (see page 23)
¼ cup sugar
1 teaspoon salt
½ cup cold shortening
½ cup cold butter, cut into pieces
8 to 10 tablespoons buttermilk

Combine first 4 ingredients in a bowl; cut in shortening and butter with a pastry blender or fingertips until mixture is about the size of small peas. Sprinkle buttermilk evenly over surface; stir with a fork just until dry ingredients are moistened. Divide mixture in half, and shape into 2 flat disks; cover and chill 1 hour, if desired. Roll each disk to ¼-inch thickness on a lightly floured surface (11- to 13-inch diameter). Place larger pastry in a 9-inch pie plate; add filling, and cover with remaining pastry. Seal edges, and crimp. **Yield:** 1 double-crust pastry.

Pear and Fig Tart

This dessert features a delightful marriage of textures between the pears and figs in the filling and cornmeal in the crust.

1	cup all-purpose flour	⅓	cup shortening
⅓	cup finely ground or sifted stone-ground yellow cornmeal (see page 23)	¼	cup buttermilk
		⅓	cup fig preserves
		2	small Bosc pears, thinly sliced
2	tablespoons sugar	1	tablespoon sugar
1	teaspoon ground cinnamon	¼	teaspoon ground cinnamon
¼	teaspoon salt		

Preheat oven to 325°. Combine flour, cornmeal, 2 tablespoons sugar, 1 teaspoon cinnamon, and salt in a bowl; cut in shortening with a pastry blender or fingertips until mixture is crumbly. Sprinkle buttermilk evenly over surface, and stir with a fork just until dry ingredients are moistened. Press dough into bottom and half way up sides of a 9-inch tart pan with removable bottom. Prick bottom of crust lightly with a fork. Bake at 325° for 20 minutes; remove from oven.

Spread fig preserves evenly in warm crust. Carefully arrange pear slices in desired pattern on top of preserves. In a small bowl, combine 1 tablespoon sugar and ¼ teaspoon cinnamon; sprinkle evenly over pears. Bake 15 to 20 more minutes. Cool completely to allow the filling to firm up a little before slicing. **Yield:** 8 servings.

pears for cooking

Bosc pears are perfect for this dessert because they have a sweet-tart flavor, and they maintain their shape during baking. Anjou and Seckel pears are also good choices for cooking. It's best to use pears that are ripe but firm.

Prune Tart in a Cornmeal Crust

David Wurth, Baker, Local 111, Philmont, New York

David Wurth, Baker, Local 111, Philmont, New York

chef's recipe

David Wurth has created a winning dessert by adding a small bit of cornmeal to a sweet cookie crust. David says, "The cornmeal is prominent both texturally and in added flavor. I tried both the coarser polenta and the finer yellow cornmeal and each works nicely—I prefer the finer cornmeal. The prunes are wonderful but if it were summer, fresh sour or sweet cherries would be fantastic, even blueberries or blackberries—all would work well. I would use maybe 2 cups of berries (pitted, if necessary, and without the steeping). At the restaurant, we serve the prune tart warm with a spoonful of ricotta cheese, and candied orange rind in its syrup drizzled over the cheese."

1 cup pitted prunes	½ teaspoon salt
1½ cups hot, freshly brewed Earl Grey or other black tea	3 large eggs
Unsalted butter, softened	1 cup milk
¾ cup unsalted butter, melted and cooled	3 tablespoons sugar
¼ cup plus 2 tablespoons sugar	1 tablespoon dark rum
1½ cups all-purpose flour	¼ teaspoon salt
¼ cup finely ground or sifted stone-ground cornmeal (see page 23)	¼ cup all-purpose flour

Combine prunes and tea in a bowl; cover and let stand 1 hour. While prunes are standing, preheat oven to 350°. Grease a 9-inch springform pan with softened butter, and set aside. Combine melted butter and ¼ cup plus 2 tablespoons sugar in a medium bowl; stir to blend.

Combine 1½ cups flour, cornmeal, and ½ teaspoon salt in a separate bowl; stir flour mixture into butter mixture. Using your hands, knead dough slightly so that it comes together (the dough will be wet). Press dough evenly into prepared springform pan, going up sides about 1½ inches. (The dough will look a bit rough around edges.) Bake at 350° for 20 to 25 minutes or until lightly browned.

Increase oven temperature to 400°. Drain prunes, and arrange evenly over tart shell. In a blender or food processor, combine eggs and next 4 ingredients; process 30 seconds. Add ¼ cup flour, and process 30 seconds. Pour egg mixture over prunes. Bake at 400° for 30 to 35 minutes or until custard is set and lightly browned. Remove from oven, and cool 30 minutes; release and remove sides of pan. The tart can be lifted off the bottom of springform pan with a long spatula and placed onto a serving plate for easier serving. Serve warm or at room temperature. **Yield:** 8 servings.

Blackerry Cobbler with Blue Cornmeal Biscuit Crust

If you're in the mood for a "comfort food" dessert, try a fruit cobbler. They're easy to prepare and oh-so-easy to enjoy. I've called for frozen blackberries so that you can enjoy this recipe year-round, but, of course, fresh blackberries can be substituted when they're available. I like to use blue cornmeal for the biscuit topping—white or yellow will be fine, just not as colorful!

¾ cup sugar

2 tablespoons cornstarch

½ cup grape juice

1 tablespoon lemon juice

2 (12-ounce) packages frozen blackberries, thawed, or about 4½ cups fresh blackberries

1 cup all-purpose flour

¾ cup finely ground or sifted stone-ground blue cornmeal (see page 23)

2 tablespoons sugar

2 teaspoons baking powder

½ teaspoon salt

6 tablespoons cold butter, cut into small pieces

1¼ cups buttermilk

1 tablespoon sugar

Vanilla ice cream (optional)

Preheat oven to 425°. Combine ¾ cup sugar and cornstarch in a small saucepan; gradually whisk in grape juice and lemon juice. Bring mixture to a boil, stirring constantly; reduce heat to low, and simmer 1 minute, stirring constantly. Place blackberries in a lightly greased 11- x 7-inch baking dish; pour grape juice mixture over blackberries, stirring gently to coat.

Combine flour and next 4 ingredients in a bowl until well blended. Cut in butter with a pastry blender or fingertips until mixture resembles small peas. Add buttermilk, stirring just until dry ingredients are moistened. Spoon dough by rounded tablespoonfuls onto blackberry mixture; sprinkle dough with 1 tablespoon sugar. Bake at 425° for 30 to 35 minutes or until blackberry mixture is bubbly and topping is lightly browned. Cool slightly. Serve warm with vanilla ice cream, if desired. **Yield:** 6 to 8 servings.

super berries

What's so great about berries? They're rich in vitamin C and fiber and low in calories and fat, but probably the most notable trait of berries is that they are rich in phytochemicals. Blackberries, strawberries, and blueberries contain phytochemicals that act as antioxidants which seem to provide protection against the development of cancer, heart disease, and other health problems.

Warm Johnny Cakes with Blackberries

Chris and Idie Hastings, Chefs & Owners, Hot and Hot Fish Club,
Birmingham, Alabama

⅔   cup whole milk

¼   cup honey

1   teaspoon grated lemon rind, divided

½   teaspoon active dry yeast

1½   cups stone-ground yellow cornmeal

3   cups fresh blackberries

¼   cup plus 1 tablespoon sugar, divided

3   tablespoons fresh lemon juice

2   large egg whites

¼   cup unsalted butter, divided

3   cups vanilla ice cream

Combine milk, honey, and ¼ teaspoon lemon rind in a small saucepan; cook over low heat until mixture reaches 110°F, stirring occasionally. Remove pan from heat, and add yeast; cover and steep 15 minutes or until yeast begins to foam. Whisk together cornmeal and milk mixture in a bowl until smooth. Cover and let rise in a warm place (85°), free from drafts, 30 minutes. While batter is rising, place blackberries in a bowl; sprinkle with 3 tablespoons sugar. Stir in lemon juice and remaining ¾ teaspoon lemon rind; allow berries to sit at room temperature 30 minutes, stirring occasionally.

Beat egg whites at low speed with an electric mixer until foamy. With machine running on low, add remaining 2 tablespoons sugar, ½ tablespoon at a time. Increase speed to medium, and beat until medium-stiff peaks form. Once dough has risen and soaked up most of the liquid, fold one-third of beaten egg whites into dough batter. Add a second third of egg white mixture to batter, and fold until well incorporated. Fold in remaining egg whites, being careful not to overmix or deflate batter.

Heat 1 tablespoon butter in a cast-iron skillet over medium-high heat. Add batter, 2 rounded tablespoonfuls at a time, to form cakes about the size of silver dollars. Cook cakes 1½ minutes on each side or until golden brown and cooked through. Transfer to a plate, and keep warm. Repeat with remaining butter and batter. Serve macerated blackberries and juices over cakes and ice cream. **Yield:** 6 servings.

chef's recipe

Chef Hastings treats every dish he serves as a work of art—it's no surprise that he was named one of the best chefs in the South by the James Beard Foundation. Chris exemplifies the many chefs across the country who present a sophisticated new approach to Southern cooking. With the creation of this dessert version of traditional Johnny cakes, he carefully considered texture, taste, and appearance. Chris explains, "Pancakes tend to be flat, not just in their appearance but in taste, too. When we think about dishes, we always look for opportunities to add texture. When you bite into a Johnny cake, it isn't quite crunchy but it reminds you that the cornmeal is in there."

Cornbread Pudding with Whiskey Sauce

Inventive cooks have always used what they had available to create some of our favorite traditional recipes. So it is with bread pudding: "Don't throw out the bread because it will make a great dessert." And now, "Don't throw out the cornbread!" This bread pudding variation is great on its own, but many think it's even better with the accompanying Whiskey Sauce.

whiskey sauce:

Combine 1 large egg (lightly beaten), 1 cup sugar, ¼ to ⅓ cup bourbon, and ½ cup unsalted butter (cut into small pieces) in the top of a double boiler, stirring to blend. Place over boiling water, and cook 5 minutes or until mixture starts to bubble around edges and sugar dissolves. Serve warm. Yield: 1½ cups.

Cooking spray or vegetable oil
1 cup finely ground or sifted stone-ground cornmeal (see page 23)
1 tablespoon sugar
2 teaspoons baking powder
½ teaspoon salt
½ cup whole buttermilk
2 tablespoons vegetable oil
1 large egg, lightly beaten
½ cup raisins

1 (8-ounce) can crushed pineapple, drained well
2 large eggs, lightly beaten
2 cups milk
1 cup sugar
1 tablespoon vanilla extract
2 tablespoons unsalted butter, melted
½ cup coarsely chopped pecans (optional)
Whiskey Sauce (at left)

Coat an 8-inch cast-iron skillet with cooking spray or grease with vegetable oil; place in a cold oven. Preheat oven to 425°. (If oven is already preheated, place pan in hot oven for 5 minutes or until hot.) Combine cornmeal and next 3 ingredients in a bowl until well blended. Add buttermilk, 2 tablespoons oil, and 1 egg, stirring just until dry ingredients are moistened. Pour mixture into preheated skillet; bake at 425° for 16 minutes or until lightly browned. Remove from skillet, and cool to touch.

Reduce oven temperature to 350°. Cut cornbread into 1-inch cubes; place in an 11- x 7-inch baking dish coated with cooking spray. Sprinkle with raisins and pineapple. Whisk together 2 eggs, milk, 1 cup sugar, and vanilla until blended. Whisk butter into egg mixture; pour egg mixture evenly over cornbread mixture in baking dish. Sprinkle with pecans, if desired. Bake, uncovered, at 350° for 40 to 45 minutes or until mixture is set and just beginning to brown. Remove from oven, and let stand about 30 minutes. Serve warm or at room temperature with Whiskey Sauce. **Yield:** 8 servings.

Coconut-Crusted Polenta Cakes with Triple Berry Sauce

For a sophisticated dessert, spoon sweetened fresh berries atop custard-like polenta cakes. (What a delicious way to add healthy, high-fiber, nutrient-rich berries to your diet!) Be sure to toss the berries and sugar together ahead of time so that the berries will be sweet and juicy when it's time for dessert.

triple berry sauce:

Combine 2 cups sliced strawberries, 1 cup blueberries, 1 cup raspberries, and ⅓ cup sugar in a bowl, stirring gently to coat berries with sugar. Cover and chill. Yield: about 3 cups.

Triple Berry Sauce (at left)
⅔ cup sweetened flaked coconut
3¾ cups milk
1½ cups uncooked stone-ground
    white polenta
½ teaspoon salt
¾ cup sugar

1 tablespoon butter
2 teaspoons vanilla extract
1½ teaspoons grated lemon rind
2 large eggs, lightly beaten
Butter-flavored cooking spray
½ cup sweetened flaked coconut

Prepare Triple Berry Sauce, and chill.

While sauce is chilling, preheat oven to 350°. Toast ⅔ cup coconut in a shallow pan at 350° for 5 to 7 minutes, stirring after 3 minutes; set aside.

Heat milk in a heavy saucepan over medium heat until milk almost comes to a boil. (Watch closely, as the milk mixture can boil out of the pan quickly.) Gradually whisk in polenta and salt. Reduce heat, and simmer, stirring constantly, 10 to 12 minutes, or until very thick. Remove from heat, and stir in sugar, butter, vanilla, lemon rind, and ⅔ cup toasted coconut; stir in eggs. Divide polenta mixture among 8 (6- to 8-ounce) ramekins coated with cooking spray. Sprinkle each with 1 tablespoon coconut.

Place ramekins on a baking sheet, and bake at 350° for 20 to 23 minutes or until set. Serve warm or at room temperature. Polenta cakes may be removed from ramekins to serve, if desired. To remove cakes, run a knife around inside edge of ramekin to release polenta cake. Place polenta cakes, coconut side up, on dessert dishes; serve with Triple Berry Sauce. **Yield:** 8 servings.

metric equivalents

The recipes that appear in this cookbook use the standard U.S. method for measuring liquid and dry or solid ingredients (teaspoons, tablespoons, and cups). The information in the following charts is provided to help cooks outside the United States successfully use these recipes. All equivalents are approximate.

Metric Equivalents for Different Types of Ingredients

A standard cup measure of a dry or solid ingredient will vary in weight depending on the type of ingredient. A standard cup of liquid is the same volume for any type of liquid. Use the following chart when converting standard cup measures to grams (weight) or to milliliters (volume).

Standard Cup	Fine Powder (ex. flour)	Grain (ex. grits)	Granular (ex. sugar)	Liquid Solids (ex. butter)	Liquid (ex. milk)
1	140 g	150 g	190 g	200 g	240 ml
¾	105 g	113 g	143 g	150 g	180 ml
⅔	93 g	100 g	125 g	133 g	160 ml
½	70 g	75 g	95 g	100 g	120 ml
⅓	47 g	50 g	63 g	67 g	80 ml
¼	35 g	38 g	48 g	50 g	60 ml
⅛	18 g	19 g	24 g	25 g	30 ml

Useful Equivalents for Dry Ingredients by Weight

(To convert ounces to grams, multiply the number of ounces by 30.)

1 oz	=	¹⁄₁₆ lb	=	30 g
4 oz	=	¼ lb	=	120 g
8 oz	=	½ lb	=	240 g
12 oz	=	¾ lb	=	360 g
16 oz	=	1 lb	=	480 g

Useful Equivalents for Length

(To convert inches to centimeters, multiply the number of inches by 2.5.)

1 in				=	2.5 cm	
6 in	=	½ ft		=	15 cm	
12 in	=	1 ft		=	30 cm	
36 in	=	3 ft	= 1 yd	=	90 cm	
40 in				=	100 cm	= 1 m

Useful Equivalents for Liquid Ingredients by Volume

¼ tsp					=	1 ml	
½ tsp					=	2 ml	
1 tsp					=	5 ml	
3 tsp	=	1 Tbsp		= ½ fl oz	=	15 ml	
		2 Tbsp	= ⅛ cup	= 1 fl oz	=	30 ml	
		4 Tbsp	= ¼ cup	= 2 fl oz	=	60 ml	
		5⅓ Tbsp	= ⅓ cup	= 3 fl oz	=	80 ml	
		8 Tbsp	= ½ cup	= 4 fl oz	=	120 ml	
		10⅔ Tbsp	= ⅔ cup	= 5 fl oz	=	160 ml	
		12 Tbsp	= ¾ cup	= 6 fl oz	=	180 ml	
		16 Tbsp	= 1 cup	= 8 fl oz	=	240 ml	
	1 pt	= 2 cups		= 16 fl oz	=	480 ml	
	1 qt	= 4 cups		= 32 fl oz	=	960 ml	
				33 fl oz	=	1000 ml	= 1 l

Useful Equivalents for Cooking/Oven Temperatures

	Fahrenheit	Celsius	Gas Mark
Freeze water	32° F	0° C	
Room temperature	68° F	20° C	
Boil water	212° F	100° C	
Bake	325° F	160° C	3
	350° F	180° C	4
	375° F	190° C	5
	400° F	200° C	6
	425° F	220° C	7
	450° F	230° C	8
Broil			Grill

featured chefs

Many thanks to the following chefs and featured celebrity cooks who helped make the recipes in *Glorious Grits* especially glorious!

John Besh, Chef and Owner
Restaurant August, Lüke, Besh Steak, and
   La Provençe
301 Tchoupitoulas Street
New Orleans, Louisiana 70130
504-299-9777
www.chefjohnbesh.com

David Dickensauge, Executive Chef
The Restaurant at Tria Market
SoHo Square
1831 28th Avenue South, Suite #110
Homewood, Alabama 35209
205-776-8923
www.triamarket.com

Gary Donlick, Executive Chef
Pano's and Paul's
1232 West Paces Ferry Road
Atlanta, Georgia 30327
404-261-3662
www.buckheadrestaurants.com

Chris and Idie Hastings, Chefs and Owners
Hot and Hot Fish Club
2180 11th Court South
Birmingham, Alabama 35205
205-933-5474
www.hotandhotfishclub.com

Nick Heinrich, Chef
Crooked Porch Bar B Que
Napa Valley, California
nickheinrich@gmail.com

Mark Hibbs, Chef and Owner
Ratcliffe On The Green
435 South Tryon Street, Suite 100
Charlotte, North Carolina 28202
704-358-9898
www.ratcliffeonthegreen.com

Clifton Holt, Chef and Owner
Little Savannah Restaurant & Bar
3811 Clairmont Avenue South
Birmingham, Alabama 35222
205-591-1119
www.littlesavannah.com

Alan Martin, Executive Chef
Standard Bistro
Number 3 Mt. Laurel Avenue
Birmingham, Alabama 35242
205-995-0512
www.standardbistro.com

John Norman, Executive Chef
Cuvee Beach Bistro & Wine Bar
36120 Emerald Coast Parkway
Destin, Florida 32541
850-650-8900
www.cuveebeach.com

Chris Richardson, Head Baker
The Continental Bakery
1909 Cahaba Road
Mountain Brook, Alabama 35223
205-870-5584
www.continentalbakeryandchezlulu.com

Mrs. Patsy Riley, First Lady of Alabama
1142 South Perry Street
Montgomery, Alabama 36104
334-834-3022
www.firstlady.alabama.gov

Angela Schmidt, Executive Chef
John's City Diner
112 21st Street North
Birmingham, Alabama 35203
205-322-6014
www.johnscitydiner.com

Frank Stitt, Chef and Owner
Highlands Bar & Grill, Bottega, and
   Chez Fonfon
Highlands Bar & Grill
2011 11th Avenue South
Birmingham, Alabama 35205
205-939-1400
www.highlandsbarandgrill.com

Brian C. Williams
Bettola
2901 2nd Avenue South
Birmingham, Alabama 35233
205-731-6499
www.bettolarestaurant.com

David Wurth, Baker
Local 111
111 Main Street
Philmont, New York 12565
518-672-7801
www.local111.com

Steve Zucker, Executive Chef
Bob Baumhower's Wings Restaurant
160 St. Emmanuel Street
Mobile, Alabama 36602
(Locations also in Birmingham (Hoover),
   Tuscaloosa, Huntsville, Montgomery,
   and Daphne, Alabama)
251-625-2778
www.baumhowers.com

grits trail map

Gristmills across the country grind and sell old-fashioned stone-ground grits, polenta, and/or cornmeal. This map identifies some favorites you might like to visit if you're traveling through the area. Or, to get the freshest, best-tasting grits possible, give one of them a call. See opposite page for contact information.

ALABAMA

McEwen & Sons at Coosa Valley Milling Company
30620 Highway 25   P.O. Box 439
Wilsonville, Alabama 35186
Phone: 205-669-6605; Fax: 205-669-0113
Online sales at www.mcewenandsons.com
and www.coosavalleymilling.com
Organic stone-ground grits, polenta, and cornmeal

ARKANSAS

War Eagle Mill
11045 War Eagle Road
Rogers, Arkansas 72756
479-789-5343; 866-492-7324
Online sales at www.wareaglemill.com
Organic stone-ground grits and cornmeal

GEORGIA

Nora Mill Granary, Inc.
7107 South Main Street
Helen, Georgia 30545
800-927-2375
Online sales at www.noramill.com
Stone-ground grits and cornmeal

Barker's Creek Mill
P.O. Box 119
Rabun Gap, Georgia 30568
706-746-6921; sales by phone or mail only
www.barkersmill.netfirms.com
Stone-ground grits and cornmeal

IDAHO

Purcell Mountain Farms
393 Firehouse Road
Moyie Springs, Idaho 83845
Phone: 208-267-0627; Fax: 208-267-1618
Online sales at
www.purcellmountainfarms.com
*Stone-ground polenta and cornmeal
(organic available)*

INDIANA

Sunny Slopes
7773 South 100 East
Lynn, Indiana 47355
765-874-2170; sales by phone and
email at deatline@globalsite.net
Stone-ground grits frequently available

KENTUCKY

Weisenberger Mill
P.O. Box 215
Midway, Kentucky 40347
Phone: 859-254-5282, 800-643-8678
Fax: 859-254-0294
Online sales at www.weisenberger.com
Stone-ground grits and cornmeal

LOUISIANA

Louisiana Pride Grist Mill
P. O. Box 281
Pride, Louisiana 70770
225-654-6131; phone orders only
www.louisianapridegristmill.com
*Stone-ground grits, polenta, cornmeal, and
corn flour*

NORTH CAROLINA

Old Mill of Guilford
1340 NC 68 North
Oak Ridge, North Carolina 27310
336-643-4783; sales by phone or mail only
www.oldmillofguilford.com
Stone-ground grits and cornmeal

Lakeside Mills, Inc.
716 West Main Street
Spindale, North Carolina 28160
828-286-4866
Online sales at www.lakesidemills.com
Stone-ground grits and cornmeal

OREGON

Bob's Red Mill
13521 SE Pheasant Court
Milwaukie, Oregon 97222
Phone: 503-607-6455, 800-349-2173
Fax: 503-653-1339
Online sales at www.bobsredmill.com
*Stone-ground grits, polenta, and cornmeal
(organic available)*

SOUTH CAROLINA

Anson Mills
1922-C Gervais Street
Columbia, South Carolina 29201
803-467-4122; online sales only at
www@AnsonMills.com
*Organic corn products, including grits, polenta,
and cornmeal*

TENNESSEE

Falls Mill
134 Falls Mill Road
Belvidere, Tennessee 37306
931-469-7161; sales by phone or mail
www.fallsmill.com
Stone-ground grits and cornmeal

The Old Mill at Pigeon Forge
3344 Butler Street
Pigeon Forge, Tennessee 37863
Phone: 877-653-6455; Fax: 865-429-2618
Online sales at www.old-mill.com
Stone-ground grits and cornmeal

TEXAS

Homestead Gristmill
800 Dry Creek Road
Waco, Texas 76705
Phone: 254-829-0036; Fax: 254-829-0122
Online sales at www.homesteadgristmill.com
Stone-ground grits and cornmeal

VIRGINIA

Wade's Mill
55 Kennedy-Wade's Mill
Raphine, Virginia 24472
Phone: 800-290-1400; Fax: 540-348-1401
Online sales at www.wadesmill.com
Stone-ground grits, polenta, and cornmeal

acknowledgments

Glorious Grits was conceived because my brother Frank, his wife Helen, and their loyal customers at Birmingham's Pepper Place Saturday Market are passionate about quality food products that enhance healthy lifestyles. Much appreciation goes to Frank, Helen, Frank, Jr. and Luke for their enthusiasm and for opening doors to the chefs whose outstanding recipes grace these pages.

One of Frank's faithful customers at Pepper Place is my friend and professional colleague, Kathy Eakin, who showed genuine interest in my early ramblings about a grits cookbook. I am indebted to Kathy and many others at Oxmoor House for their encouragement, including Nancy Wyatt who promoted the proposal and Jim Childs for his final approval. It has been a joy to work with Executive Editor Susan Dobbs, whose wisdom in cookbook publishing provided outstanding leadership to our "grits team." Kelly Troiano was an incredible editor and a delightful cohort in planning, tasting, and editing. Kelly often described the *Glorious Grits* recipes as "wonderful," and now I use that word to describe Kelly. As the book's production comes to an end, I appreciate Vanessa Rusch for her organizational skills and attention to detail.

The Oxmoor House photography and test kitchen staffs identified in the front of the book are truly outstanding professionals. The visual delights throughout *Glorious Grits* are the result of their extraordinary skills and creative culinary talents. Melissa Clark deserves special recognition for the beautiful book design—her imagination exceeded my expectations.

My deepest appreciation goes to my parents for their support during this project and always. My husband Johnny and our children, Leigh and John, were a constant and loving sounding board who discussed, tested, proofed, and ate a lot of grits! John contributed family photographs, and Leigh's sound advice reflected her formal culinary training. My sister, Ann Purdy, assisted with recipe inspiration and, as always, was a faithful listener and encourager.

The making of *Glorious Grits* has been a delight because of my fantastic family and friends and an outstanding publishing team—I'm thankful to each of them for their support and to God for the opportunity.

Susan McEwen McIntosh

Susan McEwen McIntosh with her father, Ralph McEwen, and her brother, Frank McEwen.

index

*The thought of grits, whether for
breakfast, lunch, or dinner, quite
simply gets Southern folks fired up.*

—Chef Chris Hastings
Hot and Hot Fish Club